Credit Systems for the Rural Poor in China

CREDIT SYSTEMS FOR THE RURAL POOR IN CHINA

ZHU LING, JIANG ZHONGYI, JOACHIM VON BRAUN

NOVA SCIENCE PUBLISHERS, INC.
COMMACK, NY

Creative Design: Gavin Aghamore and Frank Grucci
Editorial Production: Susan Boriotti
Art Director: Maria Ester Hawrys
Assistant Director: Elenor Kallberg
Manuscript Coordinator: Phyllis Gaynor
Book Production: Joanne Bennette, , Michele Keller
Christine Mathosian and Tammy Sauter
Circulation: Iyatunde Abdullah , Sharon Britton, Cathy DeGregory
and Annette Hellinger

Library of Congress Cataloging-in-Publication Data
available upon request

ISBN 1-56072-442-0

6080 Jericho Turnpike, Suite 207
Commack, New York 11725
Tele. 516-499-3103 Fax 516-499-3146
E-Mail: Novascience@earthlink.net

Printed in the United States of America

CONTENTS

Acknowledgments

This research is part of a multicountry project on rural financial policies for food security of the poor, undertaken by the International Food Policy Research Institute (IFPRI). The research was made possible by a grant to IFPRI from the Ministry of Economic Cooperation and Development of the Federal Republic of Germany. This support is gratefully acknowledged.

In the process of the study, we received helpful comments and advice from M. Zeller (IFPRI) and the participants of a workshop on 'Credit for the Rural Poor in China' held in Beibei, Sichuan in October of 1996, organized by the Chinese Academy of Social Sciences, Beijing, Research Center for Agricultural Policies, Ministry of Agriculture, Beijing, and IFPRI.

A large number of administrators and practitioners in the Chinese rural credit system at central and local levels facilitated the empirical research through there kind cooperation in the field studies, while Chen Ziguang, Xie *Chenghao,Wu Jingye, Li and Li Yueqin* assisted the conducts of the research in Beijing. Comprehensive research assistance at the University of Kiel was provided by Graciela Wiegand and Mingzhi Sheng for the data analysis.

Zhu Ling, Institute of Economics, Chinese Academy of Social Sciences, PR. China; Jiang Zhongyi, Research Center for Agricultural Policies, Ministry of Agriculture, PR. China; Joachim von Braun, Institute of Food Economics, University of Kiel, Germany

Chapter One

INTRODUCTION

1. OBJECTIVES OF THE STUDY AND OVERVIEW

Since the early 1980s, China's economy has achieved remarkably rapid growth. Rapid economic growth and market- orientation of the economic system places especially the system of financial services under increased pressure to adjust. Since 1985, the Chinese government has also conducted a large-scale anti-poverty program aimed at reducing and ultimately eliminating poverty. In the 1980s and 90s, the central government promoted three types of poverty-reducing policies and programs:

- preferential financial policies such as reduced taxation and increased financial assistance,
- public works programs carried out in poor areas to improve rural infrastructure (Zhu Ling, Jiang Zhongyi, 1994); and the provision of subsidized credit to poor areas to stimulate investment activities.

This study focuses on the credit programs designed to reduce rural poverty. It addresses the questions, how these programs function at present, their probable impact on the poor, and how they might be adjusted in the future in order to be more effective in a rapidly changing economic and social environment.

The credit programs designed to reduce poverty were started within the context of China's economic reforms. China's rural financial institutions had been confronted with a series of problems relating to the management of credit funds for poverty reduction. The credit programs had been implemented following design features of planned economy. Various difficulties specific to a transition period have occurred with the programs' operation. Rural non-agricultural enterprises managed or supported directly by the local governments have meanwhile developed rapidly. As rural economic and farming activities have become more diversified, there has been a rapid increase in the demand for credit.

The rationale for providing credit to poor people is to support their own efforts to create new sources of income through investment activities and to facilitate consumption. Even under normal conditions, poor people's flow of income fluctuates substantially from one season or year to another. Access to credit and savings services can help to reduce the magnitude of these fluctuations, and so to avoid adverse effects on basic consumption levels (Zeller et. al. 1997). However, banks demand securities (collateral) before providing loans. Poor people have little or no valuable assets to mortgage. Also, the provision of small loans by banks which are physically and institutionally distant from poor creditors involves large transactions costs, relative to the volume of the loans. Banks are consequently reluctant to lend to the poor. The consequence is that the poorer people are, the more difficult it is for them as individuals to obtain a loan. It is necessary to find forms of financial organization which help to overcome these access and cost problems. Designers of poverty reduction programs are thus confronted with the difficult policy issue of how to make financial service systems accessible to the poor while ensuring that financial institutions remain viable and sustainable.

In the international community, recently many institutional experiments have been conducted to make credit available and accessible for the poor by setting up various institutions, such as credit-self-help groups with and for the poor, credit cooperative organizations, and poor people's banks. Among the successful and well-known examples are the Grameen Bank of Bangladesh and the rural general loan project of Bank Rakyat of Indonesia.[1] These institutions provide micro-lending services to small farmers and poor people, and also achieve high rates of loan repayment. The experiences of these banks are a challenge for the designers of China's rural financial system. While new roles are to be defined for public and private institutions, the existing 'institutional capital' of China in the area of rural finance is to be utilized in further reforms to the extent suitable (Zhu Ling, Jiang Zhongyi, von Braun, 1996).

The general aim of this study is to provide an analysis of the operation of China's rural financial system. More specifically, the study pursues the following policy-research objectives:

---

[1] See for instance the contributions by Zeller and Hamp in Zhu Ling, Jiang Zhongyi, J. von Braun (1996).

- to explain the formation and functioning of financial institutions in rural areas, as they currently operate in the period of transformation of the rural economy;
- to assess the outreach of the financial institutions to different rural groups, with a focus on accessibility for the poor and, within this context, to explore the role of informal and household-based credit and savings systems;
- to trace use patterns of loans obtained by rural households and provided by different institutions, distinguishing between loans for "production" and loans for "consumption" and re-assessing the validity of this classical distinction;
- to assess the impact participation in credit and savings services on welfare indicators, especially food consumption;
- to examine new institutional arrangements which fit the emerging economic transformation of rural China and to develop measures for reforming rural financial institutions which will facilitate the poor's access to and effective utilization of credit.

The definition and measurement of poverty is a fundamental issue in conducting any of policy studies about poverty. Therefore, chapter 2 gives an overview on it. During the past 16 years, China's entire financial system has undergone market-oriented reform. The supply, management and utilization of poverty-reduction loans has been closely tied to the course of reform. Taking this as a basis, chapter 3 first reviews the changes in the financial sector as a whole, before examining the specific changes in formal financial institutions in rural areas. *Formal financial institutions in rural areas,* such as the Agriculture Bank (ABC) and Rural Credit Cooperatives (RCC) are the most important lenders of poverty-reduction credits. Chapter 4 describes *informal financing activities* and examines the role of Mutual Assistance Credit Groups (MACGs) and other informal systems in poor areas. The operation and effects of informal systems can be studied appropriately and comprehensively only from the *community and household perspectives,* which is done in the context of analyses in chapters 5 and 6. These chapters also analyze community and household strategies in the current system with the objective of identifying the potential offered by existing, modified, or new institutions. Policy conclusions are described in chapter 7.

2. Approach of the Study and Data Sources

2.1. Approach

Viewed from the *supply side,* the great majority of poverty-reduction loan funds are provided by formal financial institutions in rural areas (Agriculture Bank and Rural Credit Cooperatives). It is necessary to have a thorough understanding of the changing financial system in general and the rural credit system in particular before attempting to explore the operational mechanism of the special credit programs for the poor. The decisions as to how funds for poverty-reduction loans are allocated are made both by banks and by central and local governments, which interfere directly in the decision-making process.

On the *demand side,* farming families (including many of the poor) usually obtain loans from many sources, not solely specially subsidized loans. The analysis presented in this study is therefore not limited to official poverty-reduction credit schemes, but includes the rural financial system as a whole, and the socioeconomic framework in which the system exists. Also, because the structure of supply and demand for rural financial services and the principles used to allocate loan funds vary from region to region, the approach taken by the study entails a fair amount of regional disaggregation.

2.2. Data and information collection

In order to study the effects which rural financial services and poverty-oriented credit projects have on poor people, a field survey program was designed for this research, which made it possible to examine different aspects of credit supply and utilization.[2] It consisted of three elements:

1) A *series of case studies* was carried out in Pingquan county of Hebei province, Tianchang county of Anhui province, and the Gaoyou and Wuxi counties of Jiangsu Province for the purpose of rapid appraisal of the business operations of formal financial institutions in different areas at different stages of development. At the same time, farming families and credit officers working at the township and village levels where interviewed regarding loan business between informal financial institutions and households.
2) Based on this initial information, a *formal survey* was designed to study the *credit systems* at the county, township, and village levels. In 1994, a pretest of surveys was conducted in Laiyang county of Shandong province, Linhe and Ertuokeqi of Inner Mongolia (*Neimeng* in Chinese), Taihe county and the Jinggangshan area of Jiangxi Province.

---

[2] In 1993, the researchers consulted the management of the People's Bank of China, the Ministry of Finance, the Office of the Leading Group of the State Council for Poverty Reduction, the management of the Agriculture Bank of China, and other decision-making institutions at the central level. These consultations facilitated the collection of information and materials on ongoing financial reforms, the process used to allocate loan funds, the management of poverty-reduction loan projects, etc.

3) Furthermore, a household *sample survey* was carried out by the Long-Standing Observation Network of the Rural Survey System of the Agriculture Ministry. This network covers 29 provinces and autonomous regions of China. It was established in 1986, based on a sample of the 1984 national representative survey of rural socio-economy. From that sample, 10 counties were selected from each of the 29 provinces and divided into three categories representing three income groups (high, average and low). From each of the sample counties, an administrative village with average household incomes was chosen, and these sample villages and their households were made part of the fixed Observation Network of the National Rural Survey System. At present, the system covers about 300 villages with 20,000 book-keeping farm households. Each year, the accountants of each sample village and the book-keeping households administer the standardized socioeconomic questionnaires and other questionnaires intended for special policy studies, assisted by enumerators from their respective counties. This study draws upon a sub-sample from the existing network. The sample survey is biased toward the central and western part of China because the study focuses on the impact of financial services on poor people in poor regions. This paper refers to the regions studied as shown in Figure 1.1. Within the framework of the rural survey system, two or three poor counties and a county with a middle-to-upper development level were then chosen from each of the non-eastern sample provinces, while two well-off counties were selected from each of the eastern sample provinces. A total of 12 provinces, 34 counties in those 12 provinces, 34 townships of the sample counties and 34 villages from the sample townships were thus selected (i.e. from each sample

county, a township was selected, and from each sample township, a village was chosen, as shown in Figure 1.2). The number of survey households in the selected villages amounted to 1,920.[3]

Figure 1.1 Regional Coverage of Study

REGION	PROVINCES
Northwest	Shaanxi and Gansu;
Southwest	Yunnan, Guangxi, and Sichuan;
Midland	Shanxi, Henan, Jiangxi, and Inner Mongolia;
Northeast	Jilin;
East	Zhejiang and Shandong (as reference group)

Figure 1.2 The Sub-Sample Approach of the Study (proceeding from county to household level)

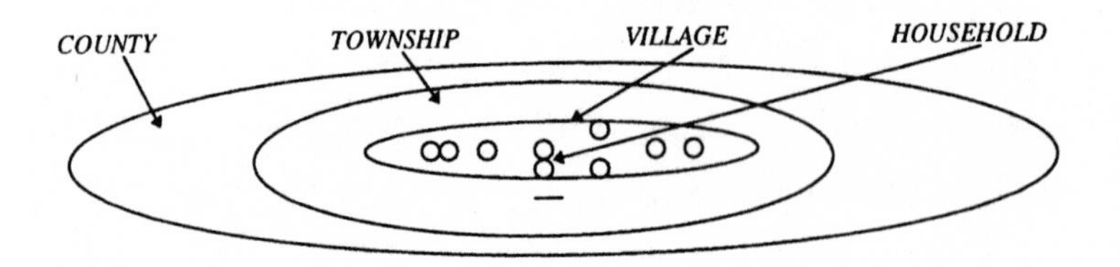

[3] The data set for the 1993 year was selected from the database in order to maintain its consistency with the period of the institutional survey. The institutional questionnaires were circulated through the Rural Survey System to the Agriculture Banks of the sample counties, the Rural Credit Cooperatives of the sample townships and Credit Stations of the sample villages. The questionnaires were filled in by the enumerators of the survey system during interviews with the loan officers of these financial institutions.

Chapter Two

DEFINITION OF THE RURAL POOR

1. POVERTY LINE

The definition and measurement of poverty is a fundamental issue in working out poverty alleviation policies. The term "poverty" used in present China, both theoretically and practically, has been in its economic sense, and especially in the sense of the absolute poverty. This can be seen from various conducts for defining a poverty line (Zhu Ling and Jiang Zhongyi,1996). All approaches are actually based on an idea that the poverty implies the individual or household whose earnings and other income cannot meet his or the household's basic needs of living.

In fact, there had been no poverty line set in China at all before 1985 when the Chinese government began to launch a massive antipoverty campaign. During the period of the People's Communes the poverty of vulnerable groups blended with widespread poverty of entire rural population and did not appear noticeable. A minimum level of per capita annual food grain consumption, 210 kilograms equivalent to 2 100 calorie intake, was used as a poverty line in a study on that period, as the calorie intake from grain consumption constituted 91-93% of the total in an average farmer's food consumption prior to the 1980s (Zhou Binbin, 1991). The study results showed that there had been 13-17 provinces in the years of 1957-76 short in food supply and 330-440 million rural people, that made 43-58% of the total population taking part in the Communes' food grain distribution, had annually received an amount less than 210 kilograms of food grain. In this group, 130 million people only obtained an annual amount less than 150 kilograms per capita food grain. They were obviously the poorest from the poor, with serious status of food insecurity.

The economic reforms begun at the end of the 1970s endowed individual farmers with autonomy in operation and eventually led the abolition of the system of the People's Communes. These significant institutional innovations gave a strong impetus to rural economic growth. Most farmers exploited the chances of raised prices for farm products, structure adjustment, and development of non-farming industries, and allocated their resources in a more efficient way. As a result, their household income grew by a wide pace in a short period and nearly 200 million people got themselves off the state of food shortage. The changes not only have helped the Chinese government to concentrate its efforts to solve the remaining poverty problems, but also have facilitated the identification of the poor still in existence. These existed by then still a rural population totaling about one-tenth of the national gross and living in areas with poor resources and fragile infrastructure, who had scarcely benefited from the reforms and were still under the menace of food insecurity. A poverty line was then set by the central government to discern the poor people, poor households and poor areas in 1985, that is: " per capita annual food grain consumption less than 200 kilograms and per capita annual net income less than 200 yuan". On the basis of this criterion nearly 700 counties were selected as the main target of poverty alleviation efforts.

2. Different Measurement

The officially-fixed poverty line was often inquired and criticized by a number of overseas and domestic scholars for its approaches, such as a lack of well-designed sample surveys, of consideration on changes in price index and on spatial cost-of-living differences, etc. Varied estimation results on poverty incidence of rural China were derived from different data sets or with different approaches (World Bank, 1992 and Riskin, 1993). However, the poverty lines defined in the theoretical explorations were not adopted in the practices.

In fact, manifold policy considerations were involved in the process of defining the official poverty line. First of all, such a criterion should be easily understood and used by the officials at all governmental levels to identify the poor for its simplicity. Second, there would be no doubt that all the counties and people identified as the poor with this criterion were of the poor stratum, since the poverty line was determined anyhow with references to the information about food grain consumption of farmers' households in the period of the People's Communes and to the research results based on a nation-wide policy study conducted in 1984. The national average of the per capita net income of a rural household in 1985 was 398 yuan. Even the households with 200 yuan per capita net income represented only the level of half the national average. Third, there were a great number of farmers households around similar low income levels and they need to be supported, but the financial resource of the central government available for this end was extremely limited, therefore, the poverty line was fixed at a level with which the size of the poor and poor areas could be confined within the capacity of financial assistance. Up to now this principle is still valid, for example, it was noticed by the author in a field study in Yunnan Province at the southwest of China in 1996, that the poor assisted with poverty alleviation programs were selected with a standard of per capita net income below 300 yuan though the national poverty line is 530. Such cases commonly exist in other poverty stricken regions while it is also not rare that the governments of better-off provinces define their poor with the income level higher than the national ones. These imply that certain extent of considerations on spatial cost-of-living differences are involved in the identification of the poor in practice.

Moreover, there were also considerations of political stability as well as regional balance of interests in the decision making process to set the poverty line, for instance, different income levels were chosen for identifying the poor counties where the minority ethnic groups concentrated and where once the former revolutionary base areas were, as specially preferential treatments. Even the finally fixed poverty line reflected the results of compromises between the central and the local governments (Zhu Ling and Jiang Zhongyi,1996), therefore, it can be considered as a "policy-implemented poverty line".

Since the poverty line was initially set in the mid-1980s, then how did the poverty incidence come out for 1978? It was actually reckoned by the State Statistical Bureau (SSB) based on estimation with the sample data from its routine Rural Household Survey in 1988. The SSB's rural sample survey covers all provinces and contains 67 000 households, which is considered a most reliable data source in present China (Chen Shaohua and Ravallion, 1995). The approach of SSB to measuring poverty was: first, to estimate a food poverty line, i.e. the food consumption expenditure of the low income groups whose food bundle could meet a food energy

Table 2.1 The Size of Rural Poverty in China in Selected Years of 1980s-90s

Years	Rural population (million people)	Head-count indices of poverty (%)	Number of the poor (million people)
1978	803	30.70	250
1985	844	14.80	121
1990	896	9.40	85
1992	912	8.80	80
1994	915	7.70	70
1995	918	7.10	65

Source: Institute for Rural Development, CASS and The General Team of the State Statistical Bureau for Rural Socioeconomic Survey (1996) *95' Rural Socioeconomic Development Report of China*, The Social Science Publisher of China, Beijing.

requirement of about 2 100 calories per person per day; second, to augment the food-poverty line with non-food consumption expenditure of those low income households based on a regression modal. This result can be considered as a "statistical poverty line" in comparison with that policy-implemented poverty line. Measured with the statistical poverty line, the rural poverty incidence was computed for different years allowing for changes in rural consumer price index (Table 2.1).

2.3 Recent Estimation

Although the SSB reported poverty incidence measured with the statistical poverty line has been widely deemed as authoritative information and it becomes now a part of officially published statistics, the SSB's approach still needs to be improved with sounder methodologies prevalent in international poverty studies. From this point of the view, the study conducted by Ravallion, Chen and Jalan on the dynamics of poverty in selected regions of south China can be taken as an important reference (Ravallion, Chen and Jalan, 1996). In the study, they reprocessed the primary data, stemming from the rural household survey of the SSB, for four provinces (Guangdong, Guangxi, Guizhou and Yunnan) over 1985-90, by means of re-valuing non-marketed farm products at prices which better reflect opportunity costs, estimating consumption expenditures as an alternative welfare indicator to incomes and adjusting for spatial cost-of -living differences. Furthermore, "poverty gap index" and "squared poverty gap index", as additional measures to head-count index which has been most commonly applied in China, were introduced for estimation on poverty deficit and poverty severity. The results of estimation indicated a tendency of changes in poverty profile similar to what was showed by the statistics of the SSB, that is, progress in poverty reduction slowed down after the mid-1980s (Table 2.1). Moreover, the study also confirmed that significant gains were obtained by the rural poor in the richer and more rapidly growing coastal regions, but low growth and adverse distributional effects slowed progress in poorer inland provinces in late 1980s.

The most recent estimation with the same three poverty measures for the year of 1995 was undertaken by the scholars from the Institute of Economic, Chinese Academy of Social Sciences (Table 2.2). Although the estimation can only show a static poverty profile because of the limitation of a snap-shot survey, it contains more detailed information about impact of public and private income transfers on poverty reduction, and it describes the poverty deficit and poverty severity for broader areas (19 provinces) than the study of Ravillion et al. As was explained by several pieces of literature that the head-count index tells only poverty size with percentage of the population who live in households with a consumption per capita, indicated by income or expenditure, less than the poverty line; whereas, the poverty gap index answers the question about extent of poverty by the mean of distance below the poverty line expressed as a proportion of that line, where the mean is formed over the entire population, counting the non-poor as having zero poverty gap; the squared poverty gap index however, as the mean squared proportionate poverty gap, gives the poorest more weights and it is sensitive to distribution among the poor (Ravallion, 1994). Based on this understanding, it can be seen from a comparison of the figures at the second row with those at the first in Table 2.2, that the poverty incidence, deficit and severity would be more serious if without income transfer. Among the four individual components of income transfers, the public transfer is of most significant for lowing poverty incidence, reducing poverty gap and minimizing inequalities among the poor (see the fifth row of Table 2.2). In this respect, the private transfer ranked at the second position (see the last row), remittance of the migrated labor at the third (the row 6) and followed by the provision of public welfare funds of village communities (the row 4). It can be then concluded that a mechanism of poverty alleviation, constituting of more or less governments action, village communities effort and inter-households assistance, has existed in rural society of China.

Table 2.2 Effects of Transfer Income on Poverty Reduction of Rural China, 1995

income type	number of poor	mean income of poor	head-count-indices	poverty gap	squared poverty gap
1	2987	359.08	8.60	0.0269	0.0143
2	3395	285.63	9.78	0.0307	0.0164
3	3316	307.51	9.55	0.0298	0.0160
4	2994	344.06	8.62	0.0270	0.0144
5	3173	323.80	9.13	0.0285	0.0152
6	3043	321.39	8.76	0.0276	0.0147
7	3092	327.78	8.90	0.0280	0.0150

Source: Rural household income survey conducted in 1995 by the Institute of Economics, Chinese Academy of Social Sciences. The sample size is 7 998 households of 19 provinces, which were selected from the rural survey sample of the State Statistical Bureau (SSB) with a stratified sample approach.

Notes: Poverty line (z) is 530 yuan in 1995, which was estimated by SSB; total sample is 34 739 individuals; welfare indicator = household net income per capita (y); poverty gap = $[(z-y) / z] / n$; squared poverty gap = $[(z-y) / z]^2 / n$; Income type: 1= net income (y); 2-7 = the amount that the following income components are subtracted respectively from the net income: Public welfare funds of village communities (PW); Public transfer of governments (PT); Remittance of family members working off-farms (R); Private transfer or income from gifts (G). 2= y- PW-PT-R-G; 3=y-PW-PT-G; 4=y- PW; 5=y-PT; 6=y-R; 7=y-G.

Chapter Three

THE FINANCIAL SYSTEM IN RURAL AREAS

1. OVERVIEW OF NATIONAL SYSTEM

When China started on the road to economic reform in 1978, there was only one bank in all of China, the People's Bank of China. At grass-roots level, several Rural Credit Cooperatives which were defined as collective financing organizations coexisted with the branches of the state-owned bank (Wu Qiang, 1990). This monolithic banking system was the result of the Chinese planned economy. To meet the requirements of the planned economy, the banking system was incorporated in governmental planning and served the government as an instrument for distributing funds according to the needs of the state. The bank also acted as an accounting agency for the state's finances. The People's Bank of China functioned both as a central bank and a commercial bank with branches distributed throughout China. Because the mobilization of savings and the distribution of credit were organized according to the plan and the interest rates were fixed by the state, the branches of the bank at the grass-roots level were neither empowered to make business decisions nor held responsible for their business dealings. Some of the important steps taken in the initial phase of economic reform were aimed at bringing about economic decentralization, separating banks' administrative functions from their business functions and giving banks more and more decision-making power. As a result of these changes, the financial sector has gradually emerged from its subordinate role in the state's financial system..

In the period from 1979 to 1983, several financial institutions were established, such as

- the Agriculture Bank, responsible for rural financial business,
- the Bank of China, in charge of managing foreign-credit and foreign-exchange business,
- the Construction Bank, in charge of long-term investment and credit and
- the Investment Bank, responsible for administering World Bank loans to China.
- In addition to the Industrial and Commercial Bank, which was spun off from the People's Bank, the Insurance Company of China was restored to handle domestic business.

Since 1984, the People's Bank of China has had only the function of a central bank. Some monetary-policy instruments used in the international community have meanwhile also been introduced in China. Basically, a central banking system has been established. (Xie Ping and Xu Jian, 1992).

Table 3.1 Institutional Structure of China's Financial System

Institutions	*Name*
Banking system Central bank	The People's Bank of China
Sectoral banks	The Industrial and Commercial Bank of China The Agriculture Bank of China The Bank of China The People's Construction Bank of China
Policy Banks	The State Development Bank The Agricultural Development Bank of China The Import-Export Bank of China
Commercial banks	Transportation Bank Industrial Bank of the Trust Investment Company of China
Cooperatives	Rural Credit Cooperative Urban Credit Cooperative
Other saving institutions	Foreign saving banks Joint-venture banks Regional banks
Non-banking financial institutions	Trust investment companies Insurance companies Accounting companies Leasing companies Post savings Stock-exchange companies

Sources: Xie Ping and Xu Jian (1992) Monetary Reforms of China, p.15, Trianjin People's Publishing House, Tianjin.

The Planning Division of the People's Bank of China (1994) Documents Concerning Reforms in Credit Management, pp. 3-9, The Publishing House of Chinese Economy, Beijing.

By 1994, in addition to the People's Bank of China, there were 4 sectoral banks, 9 national and regional commercial banks, 12 insurance companies, 387 trust investment companies, 87 stock exchange companies, 29 accounting companies, 11 leasing companies, 59,000 Rural Credit Cooperatives, and 3900 Urban Credit Cooperatives distributed throughout the country. Also, 225 foreign banks had established 302 offices and 98 business branches in China (Zhou Zhengqing, 1994). Since 1994, the financial institutions have been further divided and re-organized. First, the People's Bank no longer has to deal with loan business, but has been given the tasks of stabilizing the Chinese currency and supervising other financial institutions. Secondly, three banks have been established to deal with the policy credit business formerly handled by sectoral banks. The sectoral banks are being transformed to state-owned commercial banks (Table 3.1).

Although the credit sector has undergone the above major institutional reforms during the past 16 years (1979-1994), the efficiency of the Chinese financial system is far from what is required by a market economy. The independence of the People's Bank of China as a central bank cannot be guaranteed. The various levels of government still exert great influence on the distribution of credit. The interest rates are determined primarily through the administrative power of the central government.

At present, 90% of all banking employees work at the four sectoral, state-owned banks; these banks own 98 % of all business offices and 84 % of all financial properties, and handle 75% of China's saving and credit business. The monopoly/monopolistic position of the state-owned sectoral banks has resulted in the separation of the financial markets/has caused the financial markets to separate, reduced the efficiency of the entire financial system, and impaired the effectiveness of macro-management by the central bank. In addition, numerous state-owned industrial enterprises (which incur losses), have also impeded the transformation of the sectoral banks into commercial banks. In the mid 1990s, the sectoral banks' 2,400 billion Yuan worth of outstanding loans include at least 20% bad debts, due mainly to loss-making state enterprises (He Dexu, 1995). It is therefore to be expected that the Chinese financial system and its manner of operation must be changed further in keeping with business reforms.

2. Formal Financial System in Rural Areas and Agricultural Credit

There are three types of formal financial institutions in the rural areas of China: the Agriculture Bank of China (ABC), the Agriculture Development Bank of China (ADB) and the Rural Credit Cooperatives (RCC). These organisations shall be described briefly.

The Agriculture Bank (ABC) is structured along the lines of the national administration, i.e. is a hierarchy consisting of a central headquarters and branches in provinces, prefecture cities, counties and big townships (see Figure 3.1). Of these different levels, only offices at the county and township levels actually engage in business, while the offices at the central, provincial and city levels perform exclusively managerial functions.

The Agriculture Development Bank (ADB) was set up in November 1994 when the government decided to differentiate between agricultural policy loans and commercial loans. Agricultural loans have low interest rates subsidized by the government in order to achieve certain policy objectives. Agricultural loans may be obtained for the following purposes:

- for storing major agricultural crops and produce such as food grains, cotton, oil seeds, pork, and sugar;
- for purchasing, distributing, marketing and processing these/such products;
- for alleviating poverty and conducting comprehensive agricultural development projects set up by the state council;
- for implementing technological improvements and carrying out construction projects relating to plant production, forestry, animal husbandry, or irrigation systems (Agriculture Development Bank of China, 1994).

Earlier, most policy loans were granted by the Agriculture Bank (ABC), but now they are all handled by the Agriculture Development Bank (ADB). The branches of the Agriculture Development Bank do not yet extend to the rural areas outside the provincial capital cities.

There is a Credit Cooperative in every township of rural China, an institutional arrangement made by the central government. Each Credit Cooperative works within its township territories. Its savings and credit business is transacted by full-time credit officers or by village credit stations managed by part-time credit officers (APRACA/ESCAP, 1984).

In the rural credit sector, informal organizations also exist, but formal institutions have always occupied a predominant position. At the beginning of the 1990s, the Agriculture Bank and Credit Cooperatives controlled at least 80% of all credit funds in rural China. The funds of the Agriculture Bank are derived mainly from the deposits of enterprises, residents' savings, loans from the People's Bank and other sectoral banks, equity capital, etc. Credit Cooperatives are not entitled to borrow money from the People's Bank, but they can borrow from the Agriculture Bank. Credit Cooperatives derive about 90% of their funds from savings, of which farmers' savings make up more than 80% (Xu Xiaobo and Deng Yingtao, 1994).

There is an administratively stipulated division of labor between Agriculture Banks (ABC) and Rural Credit Cooperatives (RCC). Prior to the development of the rural non-agricultural economy, the credit business of both types of institutions consisted chiefly of agricultural loans. Most recipients of Agriculture Bank loans were units belonging to the agricultural support system, such as seed companies, food-grain agencies, supply and marketing cooperatives, and pre- and post-production enterprises, while the customers of the Credit Cooperatives were individual farmers. Since the 1980s, non-agricultural development policies have been promoted, and township and village enterprises have received more and more loans. This type of credit now makes up 2/3 of all outstanding loans by cooperatives, and 1/10 of all outstanding loans by the Agriculture Bank (The State Statistics Bureau, 1994). These proportions are even higher in well-developed regions. With regard to business loans/venture capital, Agriculture Bank is often responsible for providing fixed-rate loans/loans for fixed assets?, while Credit Cooperatives focus on loaning operating capital. Loans provided by cooperatives generally have terms of less than one year. Agriculture Banks provide all types of credit, i.e. short-term, medium-term and long-term loans.

Figure 3.1. Organizational Structure of Formal Financial Institutions in Rural China (numbers of offices as of 1993 in parentheses)

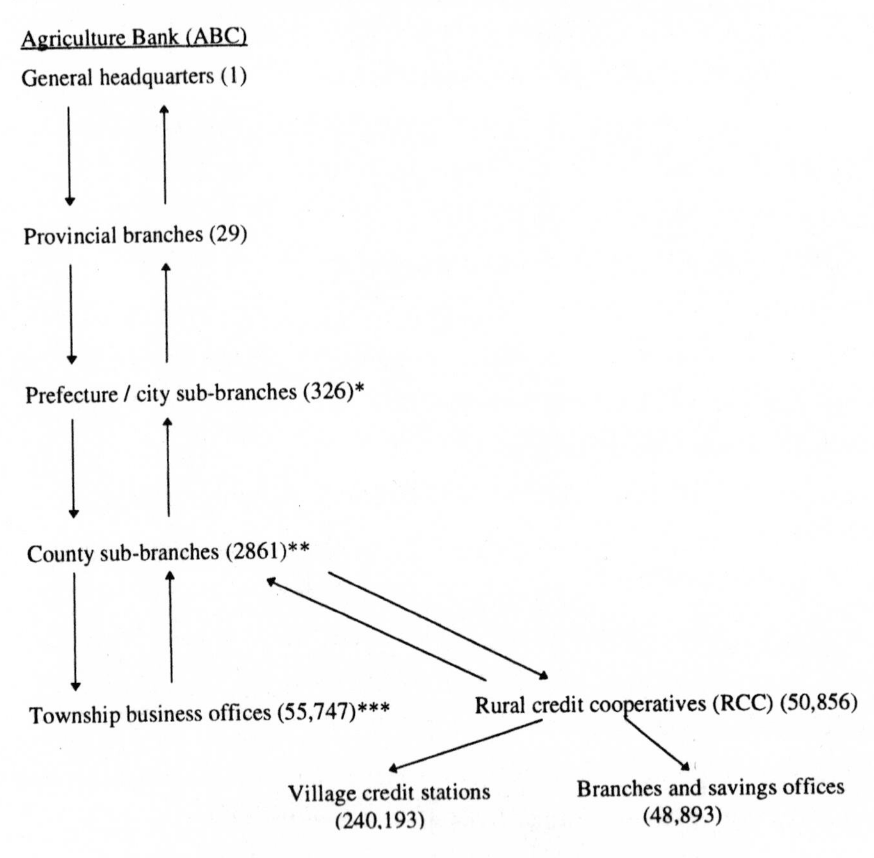

Sources: State Statistics Bureau (1994). The Statistical Yearbook of China, pp. 543, 547

*: including 14 sub-branches in the cities covered by the separate state plan

**: including 635 offices located in city outskirts

***: including 23,976 saving offices and other establishments

3. Goals, Instruments and Inconsistencies of Official Credit Programs for Reducing Poverty

3.1. Evolution of the system and problems in coordination

The fundamental aims of the Chinese government's anti-poverty policies have been to reduce regional differences in order to maintain the unity of the country and to ensure that the basic needs of low-income groups are met in order to maintain social stability. Under the existing structure, however, poverty-reduction credit programs benefit not only the poor, but also the local governments and non-poor in the poor counties. Early in the 1980s, the central government started to take action to eliminate rural and regional poverty, also through the provision of targeted credit. At that time, the financial resources were provided by the state. In 1984, the government adopted a new approach, in which additional funds were distributed with the help of credit institutions (Table 3.2). The objective of this new approach was to compel local governments and institutions in poor areas to become more efficient in their utilization of funds. Between 1984 and 1993, the central government's financial authorities and the state banks allocated 38.15 billion Yuan for use as poverty-reduction funds. Of this total, 26% was derived from budgetary funding, while 74% came from bank loans. The Agriculture Bank distributes 50% of the available credit funding (Wu Guodong, 1994) . It was just decided recently that from 1997 on the financial funds of the central government used for poverty reduction purpose would increase by 1.5 billion yuan / year, while the targeted credit funds provided by state banks increase by

3 billion yuan / year. These additional funds are to be used for financing rural infrastructure construction, extension programs and training course, development of agriculture and agricultural processing industries in the poorest areas (The Central Committee of the Chinese Communist Party and the State Council, 1996).

Basically, the Chinese government's anti-poverty scheme takes an approach of *regional targeting*. First, the central government identified about 700 poor counties, to which it then provided concentrated development assistance (Office of the Leading Groups of the State Council for Economic Development in Poor Areas, 1989a). This regional -targeting approach is used both in carrying out public-works programs and in implementing credit programs. The State Council stipulated that poverty-reduction credits supplied by the Agriculture Bank (ABC) are to be used mainly for *priority objectives set by the state anti-poverty plan*, that is to alleviate shortages of food and clothing among the poor (The Leading Group of the State Council for Economic Development of Poor Areas, 1986). Since low-interest loans to poor areas from other sectoral banks are granted mostly to county-owned enterprises which usually have no direct relation to the poor, this paper focuses on the credit programs for poverty reduction implemented by the Agriculture Bank. Moreover, poverty-reduction loans provided by the People's Bank are also handled by the Agriculture Bank (general headquarters of Agriculture Bank of China, 1987), which for practical purposes may be considered to represent the credit programs for poverty reduction in China.

Table 3.2 Source and Volume of Poverty-Reduction Funding in China, 1980 - 1993

	Program	*Annual Funding (in million Yuan)**	*Source*	*Period of program*	*Interest subsidized by:*
1	Development funds for supporting less developed areas	800	Ministry of Finance	1980-2000	(Financial allocation)
2	Special funds for agricultural construction in "Sanxi Area"	200	Ministry of Finance	1983-2000	(Financial allocation)
3	Loans for supporting old revolutionary bases, minority areas, and remote areas	1000	People's Bank	1984-2000	People's Bank
4	Special loans for county enterprises in poor areas	400	People's Bank	1988-2000	People's Bank
5	Special loans for county enterprises in poor areas	200	Industrial and Commercial Bank	1988-2000	Industrial and Commercial Bank
6	Special loans for county enterprises of poor areas	100	Construction Bank	1988-2000	Construction Bank
7	Loans for economic development in less developed areas	300	Agriculture Bank	1985-2000	(Normal loans without interest concession)
8	Specially subsidized loans**	1000	Agriculture Bank	1986-2000	Central government

Table 3.2 (Continued)

9	Specially subsidized loans for pastoral areas	50	Agriculture Bank	1988-2000	Central government
10	Specially subsidized loans	500	Agriculture Bank	1991-2000	Provincial government
11	Specially subsidized loans for state farms in poor border areas	100	Agriculture Bank	1991-2000	Central government
12	Farmland construction loans	400	Agriculture Bank	1992	Central and provincial governments
13	Loans for renovating flood-damaged works	150	Agriculture Bank	1992	Central and provincial governments
14	Loans for rehabilitating disabled poor	100	Agriculture Bank	1992-1993	China Association of Disabled, central and provincial governments
15	General loans to poor areas	500	Agriculture Bank	1993-2000	Agriculture Bank

Sources: Office of the Leading Groups for Economic Development in Poor Areas Under the State Council (1989) Outlines of Economic Development in China's Poor Areas, p.21, Agricultural Publishing House, Beijing.

Wu Guodong (1994) Research Report on Credit Policies for Poverty Reduction, presented at the International Workshop on Anti-Poverty Strategies of China, 4-7th of December, Beijing.

[a] 1985: 1 US $ = 3.71 Yuan, 1994: 1 US $ = 8.5 Yuan

[b] increased by 100 mill. Yuan/year since 1994.

Credit funding is distributed through the *administrative hierarchy* from the top down to the grass-roots level. Subsidized loans are issued by the Agriculture Bank, but the funds are provided by the People's Bank on an annual basis. The loans are repaid to the People's Bank. At the central level, the poverty-reduction office of the State Council and the general headquarters of the Agriculture Bank cooperate on planning how to distribute funds among the various provinces, based on the size of their respective poor populations. At the provincial level, the same agencies allocate the funds among poor counties (The People's Bank of China and The Agriculture Bank of China, 1986). At the county level, the credit-distribution process includes both discussions between the Agriculture Bank, the County Finance Bureau and Poverty Reduction Office and a project-approval procedure which starts with the submission of proposals at the township level (Li Jianguang and Liguo, 1992).

Poverty-reduction loans have interest rates at least 20% lower than official interest rates. The term of poverty-reduction loans is usually 1-3 years, with the longest term being 5 years. These loans are to be repaid in a lump sum at the date of maturity. In the second half of 1993, the official annual interest rate on capital construction loans with a term of 1-3 years was fixed at 12.4%, while the interest rate on poverty-reduction loans with the same term was 2.88%. The latter was adjusted to 4.7% in 1995. During this period, official inflation rates have hovered around 15%.

The decision-makers in the credit-distribution process are government institutions and the Agriculture Bank. Individual investors such as farmers have not yet entered into this decision-making process. The government and the bank exercise different functions, and the goals - including poverty reduction - of the central and local governments do not necessarily coincide (see Table 3.3). Decisions concerning the granting and distribution of loans therefore entail compromises, which are sometimes at variance with the initial intent of credit programs.

Table 3.3 Ranking of Decision-Makers' Objectives in Implementing Credit Programs for Poverty Reduction

	Ranking of Decision Makers' Objectives[a] *		
Basic goals	Central government	Local government	Agricultural Bank
Improve food security and income of poor	1	2	3
Promote non-agricultural development, increase county revenue	3	1	2
Recover loans on schedule	2	3	1

Source: The table is based on documents issued by the Leading Group of Economic Development in Poor Areas Under the State Council, the People's Bank of China, Ministry of Finance and the Agriculture Bank of China. See: Office of the Leading Group of Economic Development in Poor Areas Under the State Council (1989), Compilation of Documents on Economic Development of Poor Areas, People's Publishing House, Beijing.

[A] These rankings change over time. The situation described here occurred in the mid 1980s, when the poverty-reduction credit programs had just been set up.

3.2. Focus on enterprises, rather than on the poor

The cost of lending to the poor and the returns on poverty-targeting loan programs may be viewed differently by different levels of government and banks. This has implications for the choice of targeting organizations (e.g. enterprises) versus individual households. Compared with the Agriculture Bank's loans to individual households, its loans to enterprises and organizations cost banks less to manage. The central government's chief concern, on the other hand, is to reduce regional poverty. Since local decision-makers frequently argue that it would be more efficient to give loans to economic units to solve food shortage problems and improve the incomes of poor households, their proposals usually met with easy approval by the central government. Poor farmers, however, had no opportunity to raise their voices, and later they often lost direct access to poverty-reduction loans. In the course of program implementation, the priority gradually shifted to Economic Units for Poverty Reduction, which are defined as those enterprises or service organizations that have assumed poverty-reduction tasks. The amount of support given to these units is determined according to

- the percentage of their employees who come from poor households,
- the percentage of poor households among the total customer base receiving service from the enterprises, or
- the percentage of poor households among the rural households involved in the enterprises' production (The Leading Group of the State Council for Economic Development, 1989a).

These provisions have gradually been lifted in local programs, however, and the group of those eligible for poverty-reduction credits now includes most of enterprises and governmental departments in poor counties (Wu Guodong, 1994):

1. Production enterprises, most of which are village-owned, township-owned, or county-owned enterprises. These enterprises are intended to create jobs for the poor and to help poor households to develop family businesses.

2. Agriculture-supporting systems at township level, such as technical, extension-service stations, animal-husbandry stations, irrigation stations, etc. These stations are intended to assist poor households to participate in production projects.
3. Commercial companies which produce mainly tobacco, cotton, tea, or fruit trees, trading companies and supply and marketing cooperatives. These firms organize the participation of poor households in certain areas of production and purchase products from poor households.
4. Governmental departments such as those dealing with agriculture, forestry, animal husbandry, irrigation, aquatic production, and technical extension. These agencies set up certain production projects and organize the participation of poor households.

Most enterprises and governmental institutions took advantage of specially subsidized loans to implement their projects at locations with relatively favorable natural and economic conditions, so that the poverty-reduction loans have been used chiefly in comparatively rich areas located near towns, public ways, and factories of poor counties. The *beneficiaries of the projects* have typically not been poor households. The people who benefited most from the specially subsidized loans include the projects' organizing units, and average households participating in the projects. The poorest group of the population has almost no opportunity to enjoy the advantages offered by the credit programs.

Parallel to the change in the composition of the recipient group, the emphasis of credit use has *shifted from the agricultural to the non-agricultural sector*. In 1986 and '87, agricultural loans made up about 55% of all specially subsidized credit (Agriculture Bank, 1988). By 1993, this share had declined to less than 40% (Office of the Leading

Group of the State Council for Economic Development in Poor Areas, 1994a). A strategy of accelerating non-agricultural development may be appropriate if certain poor counties have no agricultural-resource potential, but, it is necessary to analyze the economic impact of changing the priorities of credit utilization. The cost of promoting non-agricultural development has been high for China's entire rural sector. The structural adjustment in financial systems, which has been promoted by the governments of the poor areas, has not gone far beyond the central government's policies. Certainly, the central government stresses the priority of financing agricultural projects with specially subsidized loans in order to eliminate food shortages among the poor, but the central government has also emphasized local processing enterprises. The central government also encourages poor counties which have achieved food security to develop industrial capacities which can boost the economy of the whole region and provide revenues to the local government (The Leading Group of the State Council for Economic Development, 1989b).

3.3. Policy-coordination issues and bad loans

At the central level, the Finance Ministry is not allowed to borrow money from the Central Bank. Governments at the local level do not follow this rule entirely, however, and frequently borrow money from the banks to pay salaries to their employees. The county branches of the Agriculture Bank are consequently in favor of improving the local financial structure by establishing non-agricultural enterprises. Since one of the major concerns of the bank is that borrowers provide security for loans, however, this often causes conflicts between the bank and local governments regarding project selection. Both the banks and the local governments have to compromise under the pressure of officials and the lobbying activities of borrowers. The central government applies two *criteria in assessing the implementation* of credit programs: food security and the rate of loan repayment.

A poor county was defined as being food-secure if, with the exception of 'five-guarantee households' (poor households receiving social security) and the households receiving permanent social relief, over 90% of its poor households could solve their food-shortage problems in normal harvest years. In 1990, per capita food-grain availability of 300 kilograms was considered to represent the lower limit of food security. 58.3% of the 331 poor counties receiving state assistance had already passed this threshold by 1992 (Office of the Leading Group of the State Council for Economic Development in Poor Areas, 1993). It should be pointed out, however, that most of the poor counties achieving food security are not located in the most difficult areas, and that the people who have already crossed the poverty threshold do not belong to the poorest groups. The poor who live in mountainous areas with harsh climates and poor resources are generally unable to take advantage of the relatively favorable economic conditions existing in the areas near county towns, good public roads and factories, where credit projects are often implemented. It is then questionable whether past patterns of credit distribution enabled this group of the poor to overcome their food shortages. Furthermore, certain events such as natural disasters, health problems or the influence of adverse market factors would cause groups that live just above the poverty line to fall back into poverty and could also bring the non-poor into difficulties.

The *repayment of loans* often fails to match the initial expectations of the central government. Some of the credit distributed in the 1980s became due at the beginning of 1990. Since 1991, the rate of repayment of specially subsidized loans issued by the Agriculture Bank has been less than 57%. The repayment rates of other credit programs, particularly of loans to county-owned enterprises, have not even reached this level (Office of the Leading Group of the State Council for Economic Development in Poor Areas, 1994b). In some cases, repayments are financed by new loans. Repayment may be delayed for a number of reasons:

1. Due to the direct intervention of local governments, banks cannot independently select the projects which are worthy of being financed. This has led to a number of credit failures.
2. The credit programs included many welfare components.
3. The state's over-protection of enterprises and individuals in the planned economy had created the idea that borrowers were unreliable in fulfilling their loan contracts.
4. In the current transition period, the systems for enforcing legal agreements and social contracts have been far from effective. This has encouraged many borrowers to violate their contracts.
5. A large part of marketing and purchasing activities are conducted without involvement of financial institutions, e.g. money transfers between buyers and sellers are made by direct cash payment not through banks. This makes it difficult for banks to assess the performance and operation of enterprises and to supervise the credit utilisation of borrowers.

6. The stipulated loan duration sometimes was too short for borrowers who made long term investments. For instance, loans to forestry production are provided for five years but the return from the investment needs more than seven years.

3.4. Policy implications

Given past experiences, it seems necessary to *experiment with and create new organizational forms of rural financing*. Such experimenting would combine regional targeting with individual targeting to support both regional economic development and the development of small businesses, including those in the farm economy. Such new institutional arrangements should not only ensure the poor's access to available credit, but also guarantee credit security. An even more important function of new organizational structures should be to enable the poor to contribute their own initiative and to participate actively in the entire process of setting up effective rural credit systems. This issue should be assessed further within the context of the examination of the informal sectors' potentials, which are discussed in the following chapter.

Chapter Four

INFORMAL CREDIT ORGANIZATIONS FOR AND OF THE POOR

The administrative restrictions on the credit business of Agricultural Banks and Credit Cooperatives require the institutions to pursue two objectives in making loan decisions: first, to support the state and collective economy, but not the private economy and, second, to focus on providing production loans but exclude consumer loans. When the family farm system was established, farmers' private economic activities developed rapidly. A wide variety of requests for credit ranging from production loans to consumption loans were submitted to financial institutions, but the Agriculture Bank and the Credit Cooperatives were restricted by the existing system and so could not adjust their loan policies to take into account the change in the economic system. As a result, private lending activities gradually developed in the form of some informal credit organizations, which sprang up in response to the new demands and opportunities. Some of them, such as the Cooperative

Foundations and Mutual Assistance Credit Groups (MACG) have been officially recognized and become well known. A brief introduction to the organizations providing private loans in rural areas, particularly the Mutual Assistance Credit Groups, and the activities of Women's Credit Groups, follows in this chapter. The larger 'system' of private lending between families and friends is also addressed here briefly and examined further within the context of household-level analyses in chapter 5.

1. SEMI-INFORMAL FINANCIAL ORGANIZATIONS

In the rural areas of China, especially those with a high degree of financial activity, there are a variety of informal credit organizations which differ greatly in their operational efficiency. Some did not manage well and so existed only for a short time. Some were weak in structure and still exist on paper, but are no longer active. Some have been approved by the authorities (which is why we refer to them as 'semi-informal') and become strong enough to compete with the formal organizations, and others are illegal, but have nonetheless established themselves in the credit sector. The organizations which have attracted the attention of policy researchers all over the country, however, are those which are supported by the central government or by local governments, for example Cooperative Foundations, Mutual Assistance Credit Groups and Agricultural Economic Companies. Mutual Assistance Credit Groups will be discussed in greater detail in the next section, while the other organizations are briefly introduced here.

Agricultural Economic Service Companies and Cooperative Foundations were originally established with the objective of managing the funds remaining from the production teams or brigades. These funds include the shares converted from farmers' livestock during the collective period in the 1950's and the collective accumulation after the establishment of the People's Commune (such as deposits, creditors' rights, depreciation fund of fixed assets, etc.). When the communes were dissolved and the collective assets were being distributed among the families, many villages formed village farm-cooperative foundations in order to avoid losing collective assets (Zhang Xiaoshan and Wan peng, 1991). In some provinces, similar organizations were set up at the town or township level and managed by the agricultural economic station, which was then called an Agricultural Economic Service Company (Xu Xiaobo, Deng Yingtao et al, 1994). Over the years, farm families have been paying rural communities land-use charges, public revenues and public-welfare moneys and charges, which have become the main revenues of these organizations.

With the support of the Ministry of Agriculture, *Rural Cooperative Foundations* are spreading faster than Agricultural Economic Service Companies. By the end of 1991, Cooperative Foundations had been established in 18,000 towns/townships, or 33% of all towns/townships. The number of administrative villages with Cooperative Foundations is 120,000, or 16% of the entire country. The funds collected by cooperative foundations throughout China amounted to 5,660 million Yuan by the end of 1988. The per annum growth rate averaged 20.1% Total loans increased from 6,710 million Yuan in 1989 to 10,170 million Yuan in 1991, for an average annual growth rate of 23.1%. The provinces with accumulated funds of over one billion Yuan included Jiangsu, Sichuan, Hebei, Shandong, Liaoning, Jilin, Heilongjiang, Zhejiang and Guangdong (Hong Fuzeng, 1992). One basic problem is that workers in Cooperative Foundations have not been professionally trained and lack skills and experience in financial management. Their main objective is to collect money and make loans, but they fail to give due regard to risks. This lack of expertise poses a potential threat to the security of the deposits and the sound development of the financial institutions.

In the beginning, the target groups for the Agricultural Economic Service Companies and Cooperative Foundations were farm families and township enterprises within the local community, and loans were normally short-termed. As non-agricultural investments grew, funds became increasingly scarce. Some counties and townships tried to turn these organizations holding collective funds into official local banks. Administrative structures were established at the county and township levels, and the officials of the agricultural economic administrative agencies were appointed as leaders of these organizations. Their objective is to accept deposits at a guaranteed rate of interest which is higher than the official rate and to invest these funds in projects which are supported by the government's long-term investments. The result is that individual farm families will no longer have any opportunity to obtain loans.

It is also noteworthy that a kind of *unnamed informal financial organization* appeared in recent years, that is the village *and township enterprises*. These enterprises generally do not have sufficient working capital and adopt a policy of forcing their employees to save. Each month, their employees receive a small amount to cover their living expenses, while the remaining wages are invested in the factory with the promise that, by the end of the year, the management will pay interest which is 2-3 percent higher than the official interest rate. In order to keep their jobs, the employees usually do not argue about this and regard the policy to be a regulation of the enterprises.

The types of organizations described above hardly encourage the active participation of farmers. Furthermore, administrative interference in these organizations usually reflects certain interests of some government departments. For example, some officials of agricultural economic administrative institutions regard the active foundations as savings accounts for their own interests and participate directly in managerial activities. In reality, agricultural economic service companies and cooperative foundations no longer have much similarity with farmers' cooperative organizations. With the aim of protecting the monopolistic position of their own system, the local Agriculture Banks and Credit Cooperatives made great efforts to find legal problems with the Cooperative Foundations and attempted to use the supervisory power of the financial sector to exclude the foundations from credit business. Agricultural Economic Service Companies and Cooperative Foundations are mostly located in the upper-middle developed areas, and their primary function is to administer the financial assets of collective economic organizations. They use funds for production activities within the community, and it is expected that the existing assets will appreciate. It is not part of their agenda to put the welfare of the poor first.

2. Mutual Assistance Credit Groups - MACGs -

The Mutual Assistance Credit Groups (MACGs, also called Savings Associations for Mutual Aid), which have been active in poor and disaster areas, have some potential to deliver credit to the poor. Since 1982, the Mutual Assistance Credit Groups have been promoted with the assistance of the Ministry of Civil Affairs. They originated in the Bo Yang and Feng Cheng counties of Jiangxi province, but can now be found in the poor areas of Yunnan, Guizhou, Sichuan, Hubei, Hunan, Hebei, Henan, Gansu, Anhui, Xingjiang and Heilongjiang provinces. Groups have even been set up in the disaster-prone countryside of the well-developed Jiangsu province. By the end of 1993, there were approx. 173,000 MACGs in China, with deposits totaling 1,240 million Yuan. Some of these credit groups only store food grain and are consequently called 'food grain saving groups', others function as cash depositories and are therefore named 'money savings groups', while still others collect both food grain and cash and so are referred to as 'double-saving groups'. To facilitate understanding of the following discussion, all these organizations have been subsumed under the term MACG (The Ministry of Civil Affairs, 1994). MACGs are generally set up in administrative villages. The groups' resources consist of

- the savings of their members,
- subsidies provided by the township or village collective economic organizations,
- a part of the state relief to the disaster-affected areas,
- taxation exemption granted to poor households, and
- donations from various organizations.

Permission from civil-affairs authorities at the township, county, and prefecture levels is needed to establish a group. Groups in the poorest villages also receive assistance from civil-affairs authorities when permission is granted. In the Bijie prefecture of Guizhou Province, for example, each mutual assistance group of a village is eligible to receive 2,000 kg of relief food grain and 300 Yuan as basic starting capital. Individual households can participate in the group as members. In order to become eligible for membership, a household must deposit at least the minimum amount of cash or food grain stipulated by the group. The minimum deposits vary from area to area, with the highest being about 100 kg of food grain or 150 Yuan in cash per member household and the lowest being about 15 kg of food grain or less than 20 Yuan per member.

It is not difficult to set up a credit group with support from the Ministry of Civil Affairs. The most crucial problem is how a group can become self-sustaining in its operation. Due to the low literacy rates among people in poor areas and the lack of credit-management skills within the organization, a number of groups have been paralyzed since they were established. For instance, groups were set up in nearly all of the villages of Yugan County in Jiangxi Province early in the 1980s, but only 2 groups remained in operation in 1995. The main reason for the good performance of these two is that the group leaders (also the village leaders) are dedicated to the credit business and good at money management. They are also able to impel villagers to observe loan contracts. Clearly, the question of how to consolidate the existing credit groups should become an important topic of policy studies.

Typically, group resources are divided into 3 parts: one part is deposited in formal institutions; the second part is loaned to members, and the last part is given as loans to non-membership enterprises (see Figure 4.1). The major purpose of setting-up these groups is to guarantee the basic needs of the members.

Figure 4.1 Sources and Distribution of Resources of Mutual Assistance Credit Groups

SOURCE		DISTRIBUTION
Donation		Deposit in formal institutions (Credit cooperatives/banks, food grain station, Insurance company
State relief	MUTUAL ASSISTANCE CREDIT GROUPS	Lending to group members
Subsidies by village collectives		
Savings of group members		Loans to non-member enterprises

[a] Lines indicate interest paid or service provided by the resource users

1. When the People's Communes were abolished, the social security functions at the rural, grass-roots level formerly provided by the production brigades were suddenly gone. It is not difficult for village communities in well-developed areas to collect funds for social and public purposes, but the systems of social-affair funds and food-grain reserves in many villages of less developed areas collapsed with the breakdown of the networks of People's Communes. The formation of the MACGs at least partially fills the gap

left behind by the public organizations in village communities. Completely different from the enforced collectivization movement in the second half of 1950s, the MACGs adopted the principles of voluntary participation and withdrawal. The groups inherit a tradition from the production brigades of People's Communes to make decisions on social and public affairs in a democratic way: the important affairs are voted on by plenary meetings of the members, while daily business is dealt with by a management committee elected by the plenary meetings. In contrast to the official credit programs for poverty reduction, which do not include consumer loans, mutual groups usually give priority to applications for such loans if they relate to basic needs. Areas of activity include *food insecurity and emergencies*, for instance when some poor households suffer from seasonal food shortages. Nearly every spring, food shortages occur in poor areas until the summer harvest. Access to credit can prevent undesirable coping strategies which households are otherwise compelled to adopt, e.g. to leave the villages to earn money for food elsewhere. The natural disasters which frequently occur in China not only make the situation worse for families seasonally short of food, but also cause regional food shortages. That has been one reason why farmers have voluntarily joined groups which reserve food grain in preparation for natural disasters and save money for buying food in case of need. In villages with a MACG, households which are seasonally short of food are able to achieve food security at low levels by borrowing money in the spring and repaying after the harvest. When natural disasters occur, the village committees can borrow resources from the groups to help prevent hunger among people affected by the disaster and to contribute to the reconstruction of their production capacities before state relief reaches the villages (which usually takes 1-3 months). Besides food-consumption loans, members of groups are able to get loans as soon as possible in the case of *other emergencies*, for example, to see doctors and buy medicines. Consumer loans from MACGs may also cover other items related to *important family events*, such as payment of school fees for children, purchasing clothes and blankets for the winter, renovating houses destroyed by disasters, or arranging weddings or funerals.

To a certain extent, MACGs have overcome the shortcomings of formal financial institutions regarding *loan recovery*. Most of a group's funds are derived from the savings of its members. With the explicit purpose of providing equal access to all members, the groups stipulate that individual members can borrow no more than four to five times the amount of their respective deposits. Such a limit combines the savings of the households with their loans, which positively affects the savings' mobilization. The members of a group live together in the same village community, so it is not difficult for them to supervise each other regarding the utilization and recovery of loans. The organizational advantages of MACGs are helpful for delivering public assistance to the target population. In case of disaster, state relief supports seriously affected households, which generally make up about 5% of the households affected by the disaster, while the other households are supposed to help themselves recover by securing loans. The transaction costs can be very high, and the distribution of emergency aid can be delayed if the households receiving special relief have to be identified by the authorities for civil affairs. In village communities with a

MACG, the departments of civil affairs can easily identify the beneficiaries with the help of the groups, because the whole process has been carried out before within the village community in a open and transparent way, which is easily supervised by all of the villagers.

In addition to consumer loans and relief measures, well-managed groups have also provided *production loans for the poor.* Some of the groups distribute production loans to individual poor households, while other groups hold investment shares in village-owned enterprises which provide jobs for poor households and for people receiving state relief. Furthermore, some groups use part of their credit volume to help "five-guarantee households" (the social welfare assistance system), to subsidize production on the part of families with members incapable of working, and to support the public affairs of the village communities. However, most groups have encountered problems involving a continuous loss of funds. Thus far, MACGs have had no business certification, nor been allowed to engage in savings and credit business like other formal financial institutions. Groups therefore avoid even using the concept of appropriate interest charges. Groups have to fix their interest rate below the official rates in order to show that they differ from the formal financial institutions. Under such circumstances, groups have to reduce their interest rates for savings to such a low point that it becomes difficult to mobilize more savings than the minimum deposit for membership. At present, the average funding of each group is about 7000 Yuan. A few delinquency cases and other adverse circumstances can force a group into bankruptcy. To maintain operations, some groups issue loans to profitable enterprises outside the village in order to obtain relatively higher rates of interest, but these groups are often criticized by supervisory institutions for such actions.

To sum up the discussion about MACGs, it may be said that this type of self-help group at the grass-roots level of rural credit markets is of significance to economic policy reforms and the social security system. Low-income groups have performed useful experiments in building social-security nets at the rural, grass-roots level with joint contributions by the state, village communities and individuals. Mutual assistance groups have linked villages' mobilization of savings to their utilization of credit, combined poverty reduction with disaster relief, performed effective credit supervision, and developed a model for integrating the poor in rural systems for credit service. It is therefore important to promote the rural credit cooperative movement and to extend financial reforms. It is necessary to design a legislative framework which guides the behavior of these informal credit groups, defines the relationships between such groups and government institutions, and builds the institutional linkages between MACGs and the state banks.

3. Microfinance Experiment

The principle of the Chinese governmental strategies for poverty reduction was declared as follows: (1) Food security for the poor must be put at first priority; (2) Outside assistance must be used on the basis of the self-reliance of the poor; (3) China should seek for international support but rely on domestic resource for its poverty alleviation schemes (The Central Committee of the Chinese Communist Party and the State Council, 1996). Since 1990s the international and bilateral collaborations projects have then increased in poverty reduction areas. Together with the foreign financial assistance new concept, new institutional forms and new methodologies of project management are rapidly introduced. Various institutional experiment has been going on. One of the most vigorous experiment fields is rural microfinance for the poor (Table 4.1).

The model established by the Grameen bank of Bangladesh has been introduced at the grass-roots level of rural China as an institutional experiment. The Institute of Rural Development of the Chinese Academy of Social Sciences is responsible for the implementation of this experiment (Du Xiaoshan, Sun Ruomei, Xu Xianmei, 1995). The experiment was initially financed by the Ford Foundation. Later it has drawn additional funds from Grameen Bank of Bangladesh and the Canadian International Development Agency (CIDA). Chinese scholars involved in the experiment have now named it the "Women's micro lending project". In July of 1995, a rapid rural appraisal was carried out in the context of this study at Xiling town, Yixian County, Hebei province, where the project is located. Yixian is located 125 kilometers of Beijing and is not particularly poor, compared with the counties in the west of China. The town, situated on hilly land which is not suitable for farming, was chosen at the beginning of the 18th century as the Royal cemetery of the Qing Dynasty. Now the monuments and the area are protected and preserved by state law, which also prohibits the development of industry. The average plot of arable land is just 0.8 mu in size (15 mu are equivalent to 1 hectare), however, and unemployment is a serious problem. During the lean season, therefore, the young and strong laborers go to Beijing, Tianjin, Tanggu, and Baoding to get piece-work and leave the women, the old and the weak behind to work the meager land. Since these families then lack manpower, they are rather poor. The micro-lending project gives them the opportunity to reduce their poverty, but has a value extending far beyond this because the *institutional innovation* of the experiment is helpful in improving the present system of reducing poverty through self-help credit and savings systems:

> The project spreads the concept of *"non-governmental organizations"* to the countryside. If the term "non-governmental organization" is mentioned in China, most people think of those lawless and wild mass organizations during the "Cultural Revolution", so people with the same goals will hardly join together under the aegis of a declared non-governmental organization to start their activities. The government is usually in charge of any established project, no matter to which sector it belongs. Yet the experience of the women's micro-lending groups has prompted the officials of Yixian County government and Xiling Town government to slowly change their opinion and accept the principle of non-interference in the projects. This will help to improve the rural social structure. At present, the non-governmental credit organization is named *"Cooperative for Poverty Reduction"*. Introducing the principle of management responsibility and under the leadership of a board of directors, five staff members are employed to handle the daily routine. The credit groups at the village level are the basic organization of the cooperative, and the group members are also the members of the cooperative.

It has been stressed that women are the target group of the credit services. After the People's Communes dissolved, rural economic policies were no longer designed for production teams, but for farm families or, more precisely, for the heads of families, who are mostly male. Taking agricultural technical extension and loan services as examples, the male heads of families are still the target groups for agricultural technical or management training, in spite of women's having become major forces in agricultural production. In addition, any farmer's wife going to a Credit Cooperative to borrow money must use her husband's name because Credit Cooperatives normally do business only with the heads of families, even though there is no written regulation stipulating that women have no equal part in economic decisions. Many female farmers in Yixian do not know how to go through a formal loan application procedure, but the women of the credit groups are already familiar with this procedure. The experience gained in this project indicates that if women are treated as the target group, the project can not only attract women's active participation, but involve the whole farm family as well. In this institutional experiment, the members of the credit groups are women, but those who work for the project are the whole family. In all activities such as cattle raising, sheep grazing, tree planting, etc., the husband of a group member takes part. Furthermore, when women are in the process of striving for gender equality, it is necessary to engage the husbands, too.

The local agent of the project is being trained by the experiment. Originally, some people were former employees of the county government with no special qualifications, but after their training, they immediately took part in training the participants, organizing credit groups, helping the participants to select investment projects, inviting technicians to give project guidance, traveling the country side to collect repayments and give loans, and making sure that the projects are on the right track. As a by-product of the credit program, these local agents seem to be able to reduce the government's role in development and cut down on administrative personnel.

It is noteworthy that these local agents combine the experience of Bangladesh with the local reality and make the necessary institutional innovations. Based upon the degree of literacy among the members of the credit groups, some regulations have been written down in a concise, easy-to-memorize way in a local language. The rules include not only paragraphs on borrowing and repayment, but also some social and cultural demands such as no gambling, thriftiness, respecting the old, taking good care of children, keeping harmony among family members, observing family planning, paying attention to hygiene, etc. All these principles play an active role in improving the quality of rural life. The villagers' committee was asked to take part in the management of credit groups. In the rural society of China, the villagers' committee is an autonomous organ of the highest authority and has the greatest familiarity with the village population. Without the committee's participation, the population will not accept any organizations from outside and will not feel bound by any regulations. The members of the credit groups are therefore selected with the assistance of the villagers' committees. In case a contract is violated by a member of the credit group, the villagers' committee will put pressure on that person and ask her to repay the loan. Due to the joint efforts of the local agents and the villagers' committee, the loan recovery rate is over 85%, which is much higher than that of formal poverty-reduction credit programs.

Table 4.1 - Experiment of Microfinance Programs for Rural Poor in China

Project Name	Source	Size of Fund	Project Site	Executive	Target group
Xingfu (happy) Project	Domestic and overseas donations	10 million (yuan)	19 poor counties	Associations of family planning	Mothers with below 400-600 yuan per capita annual income
Community Development	Australia government	13 million yuan for credit component	3 townships in Qinghai Province	Project Office; County Branch of Agriculture Bank	Households below 400-600 yuan per capita annual income
Integrated Development Project	Xuan Ming Hui, Hong Kong	1 million yuan for credit component	6 counties in Guangxi and Yunnan Province	Ministry of Civil Affairs	Poor households
Natural Resource Protection	Trickle-up Program , World Associate of Crane Protection	50 000 US$	6 townships in Weining County of Guizhou Province	Project Office	All households inhabited around Caohai Lake
Comprehensive Development Program	Oxfam, Hong Kong	1.8 million yuan for credit component	4 counties at South-west border of China	County Project Office and Agriculture Bank	Minority ethnic groups of the poor

In-kind (cow) Credit Scheme	Project Heifer International	1.25 million US$	10 counties of Sichuan, Xinjiang and Jiangsu Province	Local Animal Husbandry Bureaus	Poor households
Luliang Project	State Subsidized Credit Funds; UNICEF	3.8 million yuan	9 counties of Shanxi Province	Women Federations at local level	Women
Neiqiu Project	People University with German Fund	5 million yuan	Neiqiu County of Hebei Province	Economic Cooperatives of the county	Members of the Cooperatives
Qinba Poverty Reduction Project	World Bank	Microfinance component in appraisal stage	-	-	-
UNDP Poverty Reduction Project	UNDP	500 000 US$	7 counties in Sichuan, Yunnan and Xizang	Ministry of Economy and Foreign Trade	Poor Households
Microfinance Project	Ford Foundation and Bangladesh Rural Bank	400 000 US$	4 counties in Hebei and Henan Province	Chinese Academy of Social Sciences	Women

Source: Workshop on Microfinance in China, October, 1996, Beijing.

The project allows the use of an individual targeting approach, i.e. it lets individual poor households create assets and income with the aid of loans.[4] Through the Micro-lending project, each member can borrow an average of 1000 Yuan. Most families buy cattle or sheep and so have acquired a productive fixed asset besides land (this area has abundant water and grass and a tradition of animal raising). Yixian is close to several big cities, so it is quite easy to find a market for livestock products. Furthermore, in recent years the prices of beef and mutton have been increasing rapidly, and livestock-raising families can be confident of making a profit.

The Women's micro-lending project had been in operation for more than a year at the time of this rapid rural appraisal (the first loans were issued by the end of May, 1994). It is therefore still early to declare the project to be either successful or unsuccessful. So far, the total number of credit groups is less than 100. The membership numbers around 500. The research workers and international organizations view them with special attention. If these external conditions are removed, how long will the credit groups continue to exist, and will women from poor households continue to be the target group?. In resource-poor areas far from the market, that is, in China's main poor areas, it will not be as easy to select investment opportunities as it was in Yixian. If similar credit groups are established, will the rate of the loan repayment be as high as in Yixian? The experiment should continue, and the project should be expanded in order to gain experience regarding the further extension of the approach.

---

[4] In an area where the man/land ratio is tight or the soil is meager, many people cannot rely on plant production for subsistence. Even in Yixian, the authors have seen poor families who have almost nothing except a cooking stove and live without a table or chair. The members of the credit groups are mostly from such poor families.

4. Private Credit Between Family and Friends

Because the banks (ABC, RCC) have followed some of the regulations inherited from the period of the People's Communes that collective economy should be put first with credit support, not much attention is paid to making loans to individuals. When these formal financial organizations gradually become commercial banks, their services improve, but they still pay little attention to individual lending, so private loans continue to exist. Since the early 1980s, only one third of farm loans have been borrowed from formal institutions, while the rest were obtained through private channels (Policy Research Office of the Central Committee of the Chinese Communist Party and the Office for Rural Fixed Observation Spots under the Ministry of Agriculture, 1992). Private loans, i.e. borrowing from relatives and friends or from other private sources, are still common in China. In rural communities, most farm families use this method to acquire funds. Even in the cities, individuals usually borrow money from their relatives or friends, for instance to buy vehicles, or to start a shop or trade.

Consumer loans are used by farm families mainly to construct houses and create other fixed assets for non-productive use, or to cover financial demands in major family crises such as medical payments, or marriage or funeral expenses (Zhu Ling and Jiang Zhongyi, 1994). Such loans possess traditional features of *mutual aid*, for example, farmer A is going to construct a house and borrows money from farmers B, C, and D. Some years later, B is going to build a house, and A will join the lender's group with C and D to lend money to B. This is equivalent to a savings and loan group which rotates among neighbors, or we could say that it is just a fund for constructing houses. Loans of such types are also set up for medical care, marriage and funeral expenses and can also be considered an *insurance system*. Private consumer loans usually yield no cash interest, but the individuals in the loan group usually render services (if the lender needs such services) in addition to meeting the obligation to repay the loan for the sake of other borrowers. For example, in the busy season, the borrower might help the lender by working free of charge. This is the most frequent type of economic relationship in rural communities.

Farm families generally use *production loans* for investing in fixed assets and trading activities. The rate of interest for such loans reflects the local availability of funds and is decided by the degree of risk involved. For instance, the rate of interest for production loans is approximately two to three times higher than the official rate of interest, while the rate for speculative trading loans might be as much as five times higher. The monthly interest will be at least around 50%. Of course, terms-of-trading loans are shorter, usually from one to three months in length. In addition, even now, there are private production loans which demand no interest, and depend upon private relationships and local customs and conventions.

Farmers who obtain loans from other farm families generally repay their debts. Because the lenders and borrowers generally live in the same community, any person who breaks a contract will face consequences such as being blamed or ostracized by the other members of the community, and will henceforth be unable to borrow any more money from his neighbors or relatives. Borrowers will most likely accept the traditional, ethical, and moral restrictions in order to avoid being isolated. Besides, the lender and borrower usually know each other quite well (symmetrically informed), and the lender usually lends money with the confidence that the money will be returned. Since they can meet everyday, the loans are monitored at little or no cost (Lin Yifu, 1992). For all these reasons, the repayment of loans is taken more seriously in the informal credit sector than in the formal sector.

5. Some Conclusions

As the rural economy becomes more market-oriented and informal credit activities expand, the various informal credit organizations will gain a stronger position beside the strong network of Agriculture Banks of China and the township Credit Cooperatives. Some of the informal organizations are the result of farmers' own initiatives. Compared with formal institutions, the informal organizations in the field of micro-lending have the advantages of low transaction costs, flexibility and convenience for clients. In addition, each category of informal credit organization possesses some special functions, such as providing services to collective enterprises, helping people to carry on following a natural disaster, and alleviating poverty, all of which are functions which supplement the formal institutions. If the reduction of poverty and relief from the effects of natural disasters are taken into consideration, MACGs using the individual targeting approach to supply credit service to poor people seem more efficient than formal credit institutions. Yet the greatest shortcoming of these institutions is that, thus far, they are not sustainable. This is due to

- the present legal framework, which is unfavorable for their long-term operation (such as not allowing them to absorb deposits, forbidding them to offer market interest rates, etc.). Informal institutions are therefore always short of funds.
- lack of code of behavior for members. Many organizations have failed due to their leaders' abuse of power, or because individual members violated their contracts.
- lack of members professional training. They are often not competent to manage credit business and are hardly able to take financial risks into account.

These shortcomings relate partly to some government branches' direct control of the informal credit organizations. However, some of the organizations appeal to the government officials for their support. Most existing informal credit organizations are therefore indirectly closely related or supervised by formal and governmental organizations. It is worthwhile to note that some attempts have been made to form non-governmental credit systems. The appearance of non-governmental organizations is the consequence of society's tendency towards diversification. As the people's material, ideological and cultural life becomes richer, society can no longer simply be administrated by the government. Many activities conducted by civil society may operate more efficiently. For a government acting in the general interest of the public, it is still impossible to satisfy the diverse special demands of all the people. People want to express their own will in social, economic and political decision-making processes. To this end, groups of people will try to form new organizations in order to realize their interests. In addition, people of different occupations, different income strata and different religions who are concerned with the same affairs will work together in such fields as environmental protection, poverty reduction, rural development, etc. All that underlines the need for strengthening the adoption of concepts of *participation* by the public. For informal credit organizations, it is necessary to enact specific laws which regulate their conduct, but also allow them to exist freely parallel to the formal credit organizations in order to improve rural credit services.

It is also essential that agricultural extension systems extend their services to the informal credit organizations in order to assure the success of agricultural investment projects conducted by borrowers' families. Also, considering the low literacy rate and the lack of management skills among poor people, poverty-reduction programs should be designed to include and mobilize the *participation of educated people.* This approach was very much emphasized and successfully applied by the early rural savings and credit cooperatives in Germany (Raiffeisen 1970). Local agent groups are more appropriate than any external organizations to train and help the poor to make the best use of credit services, but these local agents are in need of training as well.

Chapter Five

ANALYSIS OF FORMAL CREDIT ACTIVITIES IN RURAL AREAS

Based on the sample data, this chapter will provide an overview of the availability of formal credit services. The chapter starts with an examination of the business activities of formal credit institutions in the survey counties, townships and villages and then proceeds to analyze the behavior of lenders and borrowers ,with a focus on loan-recovery problems.

1. INTRODUCTION TO THE COUNTIES STUDIED

The prosperity of formal credit business in rural areas is closely related to local socio-economic development. In order to observe and compare the operation of credit institutions in different areas, the 34 counties surveyed are classified into three groups (Table 5.1):

- the four counties of Zhejiang and Shandong provinces constitute a reference group,

- while the remaining 30 counties are divided into two groups, based on the per capita net income of farm families in 1993 (with 600 Yuan as the threshold).

Table 5.1 List of Counties in Survey*

Low-Income Group		*Middle-Income Group*		*High-Income Group*	
Province	*County*	*Province*	*County*	*Province*	*County*
Yunnan	Huize	Guangxi	Longan	Shandong	Laiyang
Jilin	Tongyu	Shanxi	Linyi	Shandong	Rongcheng
Yunnan	Wuding	Gansu	Wuwei	Zhejiang	Shaoxing
Yunnan	Lancang	Sichuan	Gulin	Zhejiang	Yinxian
Gansu	Huining	Shaanxi	Pucheng		
Henan	Xincai	Shaanxi	Zhouzhi		
Gansu	Linxia	Jilin	Da'an		
Guangxi	Tianlin	Henan	Anyang		
Shanxi	Liulin	Jiangxi	Shangrao		
Shanxi	Pingshun	Jiangxi	Taihe		
Shaaxi	Hanyin	Jiangxi	Jiujiang		
Sichuan	Fengjie	Jilin	Lishu		
Sichuan	Jiange	Sichuan	Baxian		
Henan	Taiqian	Neimeng	Tongliao		
		Neimeng	Linhe		
		Guangxi	Yulin		

* Among 30 sample counties selected from the center and west of China, those with farmer households having per capita net incomes higher than 600 Yuan in 1993 are defined here as middle-income counties, while those with farmer households having an income level lower than 600 Yuan are classified as the low-income group. The high-income group in the sample consists of four counties selected from the two provinces of Zhejiang and Shandong in the east of China.

It was known before the sample survey was conducted that these counties in Zhejiang and Shandong have long been in the high-income strata, while the net income of farm families in the western region is only 1/2 to 2/3 of the national average (Policy Research Office of the Central Committee of the Chinese Communist Party, and Office of Rural Long-Standing Observation Network, the Ministry of Agriculture, 1992). In 1993, the average per capita net income of farm families in China was 922 Yuan. Taking 600 Yuan as an income criterion yields a rough division of poor and non-poor counties in the mid-western part of China. The statistical results obtained from the sample data verified the above assumption: the average net per capita income of families was only 406 Yuan in the low-income counties, amounted to 1,080 Yuan in the mid-income counties, and jumped to 2,270 Yuan in the high-income counties (Table 5.2).

Of course, a farmer's income is not sufficient to reflect the general conditions of the counties in the sample. The ratio of population to land resources and the structures of production and employment reflect the economic features of the counties sampled from different perspectives. From Table 5.2 it can be seen that, in the mid-high income counties with a large population and little land, the township enterprises have been the greatest contributor to gross production. The internally and externally employed laborers of the counties in the non-agricultural industries make up a considerable share in these cases. Especially in the high-income counties, employees in the non-agricultural sectors make up more than 3/4 of the total labor force. Considering the fact that the increase in the income of farmers' families since the mid-1980's has been derived

Table 5.2 Profile of Sample Counties and Density of Credit Services, 1993*

Items	*Low-income counties (n = 14)*	*Middle-income counties (n = 16)*	*High-income counties (n = 4)*
Per capita GNP (Yuan)	1,300	5,800	21,000
Per capita net income of farmers' families (Yuan)	406	1,080	2,270
Population density (Persons / per km^2)	200	500	600
Per capita farmland (Mu)**	1.43	1.14	0.8
Of which: township enterprises (%)	40	47	47
agriculture (%)	44	37	29
Non-agricultural labor/ total rural labor (%)	24	36	76
Density of Credit Cooperatives (number/per township)	1.00	1.00	1.01
Density of credit stations (number/per village)	0.22	0.42	0.66
Density of informal credit organizations			
number/per township	0.01	0.03	0.003
number/per village	0.01	0.15	0.25

[a] This table and all the following figures and tables with the exception of those citing special references are based on information collected in the authors' sample survey.

[b] 15 Mu = 1 hectare

mainly from the non-agricultural sector, the differences in the economic structures of the sampled counties may be attributed to a great extent to regional differences (Institute for Rural Development, Academy of Social Sciences, and division of Rural Socioeconomic Statistics, State Statistics Bureau, 1994).

The difference in the density of distribution of formal credit institutions at the grass-roots level of counties with different degrees of development is small (Table 5.2). The densities of township Credit Cooperatives in high-income counties and low-middle-income counties showed no significant difference. This is due to the fact that Credit Cooperatives are established based on the divisions of administrative areas. Every town/township in China has a Credit Cooperative. Such distribution is the result of government interference. At the village level, however, the density of credit stations and informal credit organizations varies markedly in the three groups of counties sampled. This is because township Credit Cooperatives decide where village credit stations are to be established based on their profit expectations. As a result a credit station might be shared by two villages in the mid-high-income counties, but by five villages in the low-income counties (Table 5.2). This means that the farm families of the mid-high-income counties receive better financial services and their financial activities are more prosperous.

2. ABC County Branches and Agricultural Supporting System

As described above, monetary services in the Chinese countryside are provided by the Agriculture Bank of China (ABC) and the Rural Credit Cooperatives (RCC), as stipulated by the government. Each county seat has an ABC county branch, which is generally called a

"County Agriculture Bank". ABCs have their business offices in bigger cities and towns, but do not extend their services down to the townships, where it is the RCCs that run financial business, with farmer households being their main clients. ABCs and their business offices deal with the savings accounts of the farmers and city and town inhabitants. A considerable proportion of individuals' deposits are from farm households, besides those from inhabitants in cities and towns (Table 5.3). Empirical estimates based on

Table 5.3 ABCs' Deposit and Loan Structure at the Close of 1993

Items	*Low-income counties (n = 14)*	*Middle-income counties (n = 16)*	*High-income counties (n = 4)*
Deposits (millions of Yuan)	66.51	275.05	620.48
of which: individuals (%)	51	62	70
enterprises (%)	18	10	10
others (%)	31	33	21
Per capita deposit of the county (Yuan)	175	354	775
Outstanding loans (millions of Yuan)	156.91	426.60	589.84
of which: county-owned enterprises (%)	18	12	37
grain bureau (%)	22	31	18
private enterprises (%)	2	3	12
agriculture (%)	29	15	13
others (%)	10	22	13

* Source: This table and all the following figures and tables with the exception of those citing special references are based on information collected in the authors' sample survey.

surveys in sample counties showed that at least 50% of ABC deposits, including those transferred from township RCCs, are from farm households. ABC loans are *not* extended to farm households. In 1993, almost 2/3 of the Agriculture Banks of the sampled counties (22 banks) obtained credit funds for poverty reduction. They all belong to the low-middle-income group as defined above. On average, each county secured funds equivalent to 1/5 of the average deposit balance of the ABCs in the low-income counties. According to government regulations, ABCs can give loans only to state-owned and collective enterprises, large rural enterprises, and government-department undertakings. ABCs also exercise a control function and supervise the RCCs' activities. Due to poverty-reduction activities during the past ten years, the ABC has become the most important financial institution in China for *distributing poverty-reduction funds*. Its main borrowers are:

1. State-owned and collective agro-enterprises including seed companies, breeding farms, aquatic products companies, forestry centers, etc.;
2. Government departments or undertakings as representatives of agricultural development projects launched by county governments;
3. County grain bureaus which exercise both the function of enterprises and of government organs and are responsible for the purchase, sale, storage and allocation of food grains (the biggest clients of ABC loans);
4. Supply and sales cooperatives which, being trading enterprises in the countryside, supply farm households with fertilizers, farm chemicals, building materials, and all kinds of daily necessities. These cooperatives also buy farm products from farm households.

Thus, ABC services are closely related to the agricultural support system. Due to policy regulations, however, ABCs have long failed to support the operations of private enterprises. Although the relevant policies have become more flexible in recent years, the business relations of ABCs with private enterprises are still very limited.

Bad loans are one of the reasons for the scarcity of credit funds. In all of the counties sampled except for Shaoxing, Ningxian of Zhejiang province and Rongcheng of Shandong province, the ABCs were affected by the volume of loans in arrears. From 25% to 88% of the loans are bad, and this represents a serious deficiency in the safety of the credit funds. County enterprises and bureaus of grain, supply and marketing cooperatives absorb a large part of the funds. In the counties sampled, the above three categories of enterprises are great debtors which held funds over a long period. Even if these enterprises apply for a short-term loan, they use it again and again, i.e. as a medium- or long-term loan. Most of the ABCs are troubled by delinquency problems.

3. The Operation of Rural Credit Cooperatives (RCC)

RCCs have been established according to the administrative districts of townships and towns. It is stipulated that RCCs may receive deposits from farmer households, industrial and commercial enterprises, administrative departments and public organizations only within the limits of their respective townships or towns. Likewise, RCC loans are also subject to the same regional restraints. There is also a rule that RCC loans may be used only for production and trade purposes and have a term of no more than one year.

RCCs must ensure that loans lent to farm-households are used for the purchase of farm inputs (seeds, fertilizers, plastic films, diesel oil, etc.) and not for consumption and social expenditures. Table 5.3 shows the deposit and credit structures of RCCs in 34 sample townships. RCCs' deposits come mostly from farm-households, while their debtors are primarily rural enterprises. This phenomenon is caused first of all by the gap between the scopes of business

Table 5.4 RCCs' Deposit and Credit Structure in Sample Townships, Close of 1993

Items	*Low-income townships (n = 14)*	*Middle-income townships (n = 16)*	*High-income townships (n = 4)*
Deposits (millions of Yuan)	2.69	21.62	82.54
Of which: farm households (%)	71	79	77
township enterprises (%)	4	13	16
private enterprises (%)	14	4	2
others (%)	11	4	5
Per capita deposits (Yuan)	113	786	2 827
Outstanding loans (millions of Yuan)	1.87	18.05	82.12
of which: township enterprises (%)	13	42	84
villagers' committees (%)	1	10	9
farm households (%)	67	15	4
others (%)	19	33	3

Source: This table and all following figures and tables with the exception of those citing special references are based on information collected in the authors' sample survey.

of farm households and of rural enterprises. Another cause is that the interventions of township governments and village committees tends to influence the RCCs to lend their money to rural enterprises. Although loans lent directly to township governments and village committees make up only a small percentage of all loans, their borrowing behaviors are usually influenced by rural enterprises.

On average, RCCs' credit balance is equivalent to 82.7% of their deposit balance. The ABC stipulates that RCCs be obligated to transfer part of their deposits and deposit reserves to ABCs, the amounts of which differ from place to place, but have generally ranged between 15 and 22%. This has enabled the ABCs to 'fill the gap' between their loans and their deposits and support their credit services.

Table 5.5 Credit Ceilings of RCC in Sample Townships, 1993

	RMB 1,000-5,000	RMB 5,000-10,000	RMB 10,000-30,000	RMB 30,000 and above	Unclear *	Sum
Number of township RCCs	14	7	7	4	2	34
Percentages (%)	41.2	20.6	20.6	11.8	5.8	100.0

[a] Data is not available.

Table 5.5 shows that 62% of the township RCCs have a credit ceiling below RMB 10,000, and 41% of them a ceiling below RMB 5,000. According to business rules, RCCs are not allowed to grant more than one loan to the same borrower. There are only two RCCs in all the sample townships which have their credit ceilings topped to RMB 150,000 and therefore possess the capability to make larger investments. Both RCCs are located in developed coastal regions of eastern China. This indicates that the economic environment of most RCCs is based mainly on traditional farming, where only a number of small processing factories and retail stores occasionally need bigger loans. In this situation, the credit ceilings stipulated for RCCs are basically appropriate to the local conditions. However, if larger credits extending beyond the stipulated ceilings are required, the RCCs involved must report the situation to the ABC and apply for approval. Restrained as they are both by the realities of local economic development and by the ABC credit plan, township RCCs have long had surplus deposits.

If RCCs were allowed to develop their services beyond the limits of their respective townships and have their fields of operation widened, the present layout of one RCC in each township and the present mode of circulation of credit capitals would be changed completely. The current structural disposition of RCCs results from the previous system of the planned economy. At present, the technical means used by the Credit Cooperatives are still lagging behind, with limited business dealing only with deposits and loans, neither participating in establishing accounts for the farm families, nor remittance or transferring accounts for the public sectors. The cooperatives are therefore not like rural credit institutions in a market economy, but are closely related to the enterprises and the inhabitants. However, in the process of the market transition, it is necessary to promote cooperation between farmers in production, purchasing and marketing, and to combine this with functional credit cooperation. This is an important step in helping Credit Cooperatives to adapt to the market economy.

Table 5.6 Credit Structure of Sample Townships

	Rural enterprises	Village enterprises	Farm households	Farm-households' credit structure		
				Farming	Animal husbandry	Industry/trade/transportation
A. **Poor with per capita income less than RMB 600 in 1993**						
Percentages	13.2	1.3	66.6	50.5	14.6	24.1
Farm-household debtors	./.	./.	./.	14.5	2.0	0.9
B: **Nonpoor with per capita income above RMB 600 in 1993**						
Percentages	71.9	10.0	14.6	50.5	12.6	20.4
Farm-household debtors	./.	./.	./.	14.5	2.0	0.9

Table 5.6 reveals different credit orientations of township RCCs. Loans extended to rural enterprises and village committees have taken a much bigger share in the higher income townships, reflecting the importance of rural enterprises in promoting the economic development of those areas. The survey also shows that the composition of production loans (used for crops, animal husbandry, trade and transportation, etc.) of the farm households in the three groups of the sample townships are more or less the same, while the share of farm households taking production loans is much lower in the high-income group than in the low-income group. This may indicate that farmers with relatively high incomes prefer to use their own funds or to secure money through friends and relatives to meet their production expenditure requirements. In poor areas, 45.7% of farm households are RCC debtors, showing that they are highly dependent on RCC loans.

4. The System of Village Credit Stations

Township RCCs' have two alternatives for conducting their business in the countryside. One is to provide direct deposit and credit services throughout the *township area,* with several *full-time credit officers,* each being in charge of the business in a number of villages. The credit officers know the situation of the borrowers through village committees, and application forms for credits must have the signed approval of the village head. Village committees are also responsible for the repaying the debt on time. The second alternative is to establish *village credit stations,* whereby each credit station serves one or more villages. Each village credit station has a part-time credit officer selected from among the farmers to perform the job of dealing with farmers' deposits and small loans without guarantees. A credit officer also bears the responsibility of obtaining repayments, and his or her payment is drawn from the station's earnings through interest rate differentials according to set proportions. The part-time officers know the local situation very well and are well-informed on the backgrounds of almost everyone in the area. As a result, they easily establish business relationships with local inhabitants, and the cost of operation is much lower than the cost of transactions made through the village committees. This can be shown by comparing the following two cases (see boxes). By comparing the first two cases it is easy to see that the transaction costs incurred when the village committee acts as the intermediary are much higher than those charged by village credit stations. The third case shows that the involvement of the head of the village in the affairs only complicated the otherwise very simple matter of securing credit. It had turned the ordinary lending and borrowing business into an important bargaining position for the village committee in the village's social and economic affairs. Thus, it seems that by comparison, the village credit station is more efficient in managing credit relationships.

On average, each credit station has a yearly reward (money drawn from deposit-credit interest differentials according to a set proportion, in addition to money awards given by township RCCs) of 2,200 Yuan, which has been sufficient to encourage the credit assistants to work seriously. A village credit station is usually located in a farmer's house and can easily start up operations equipped only with a simple calculator, a small safe for cash deposits, some stationary, and a part-time credit officer with basic training in credit business. The amount of capital investment needed is relatively low. The credit officers' ages, education backgrounds and work experience as shown in Table 5.7 suggest that they are basically competent for the job. All these factors combined make up a fundamental condition for the successful operation of village credit stations.

Case 1: Qi Jianhong, a farmer in Meigang Village of Yugan County, borrowed RMB 400 Yuan from the village credit station to buy chemical fertilizer with a monthly interest of 1.8% and a maturity length of 8 months. The standard monthly interest at that time was set at 0.915%, with township RCCs having the right to float it upward by up to 60%. Thus, the credit station in Meigang village had violated the regulation by granting the loan at the interest of 1.8%, and Qi Jianhong had to pay 10.75 Yuan more than normally required. However, due to the small size of the amount, Qi accepted the loan. Yet another condition imposed by the station was that 10 Yuan must be deducted from every 100 of the loan as a mortgage fund. What Qi Jianhong really received therefore was a loan of 360 Yuan instead of 400, and he still had to pay the interest for the deducted 40, an amount of 5.76 Yuan. It meant that, altogether, Qi had made an additional payment of 16.5 Yuan (10.75+5.76) as the cost for a loan of 360 Yuan. However, the work had been done smoothly, with the whole process taking only 20 minutes. Asked why he didn't go to the township RCC for the required loan, Qi replied that he had no friends there and was afraid of being refused. Furthermore, he added, even though the loan would possibly be approved there, he would not like to have to go to the trouble of traveling to and from the township RCC at least twice. So, he said, it was the better choice to have the problem solved in the village.

Case 2: A farmer named Zhang Ziyan lived in Taihe County's Fenghuang Village, where no village credit station was available. Last year, the farmer borrowed RMB 400 Yuan to buy fertilizer and seeds for a term of one year at a monthly interest of 1.5%, which was in accord with the regulations. However, he repaid only 200 Yuan when the loan was due, so that he had to pay a fine of 3.6 Yuan every month. This year, Zhang Ziyan applied for a new loan of another 400 Yuan, which needed the village head's approval written on the application form. He managed to meet the village head only after paying two visits to the latter's house. The village head was reluctant to give his consent at first. He changed his mind later on and signed the form finally after Zhang's repeated requests. "Now I have shown due respect for your feelings. You must repay the amount in arrears as soon as possible," he said to Zhang on that occasion. After that, Zhang went to the township RCC to make the application formally. He got the loan only after visiting the RCC office twice on two successive days. However, 50 Yuan was deducted as part of the payment for arrears. Zhang was asked, when receiving the loan, if he would like to repay the favor of the village head. He replied with "yes". Later on, Zhang worked 3 days without pay on the construction of the village head's house, equivalent to 24 Yuan in value according to local labor prices. Indeed, the transaction cost that incurred to Zhang should include at least two items: (1) 24 Yuan of his three-day labor cost to repay the favor done by the village head; and (2) the time consumed by Zhang's repeated visits to the persons involved.

Table 5.7 Profile of the Village Credit Stations in the Survey*

Items	Low-income villages (n = 8)	Middle-income villages (n = 9)	High-income villages (n = 5)
Average number of households in village	257	414	378
Deposit per credit station (1000 Yuan)	276	635	4.122
Average percentage of the households with deposit in a village (%)	39.7	58.5	86.5
Outstanding loans (1000 Yuan)	14	136	676
of which: production loans (%)	85	85	100
Average percentage of households with loans in a village (%)	52.9	37.7	32.8
Minimum loans of a household in the survey year (Yuan)	34	49	1100
Loan repayment rate (%)	61.7	56	48.4
Percentage of households with loans in arrears over 2 years (%)	27.7	44	42.5
Averages of credit officers:			
ages	40	32	26
years of schooling	5.5	10.6	9.3
years of credit work experience	15.5	n.a.	4.7
Percentage of female credit officers (%)	13	36	100

* Includes only the sample villages containing a credit station

n.a. = Data not available

The 34 sample townships are divided into two groups according to whether or not they contain a village credit station (26 townships with stations and 8 without) and compared to show the impact of the stations (see the first two columns of Table 5.8). Per village deposit amounts in villages with credit

Table 5.8 Credit Operations in Villages With and Without Credit Stations

Per village deposits of farm households in each type of townships		Per village (with per capita net income less than 600 Yuan) rate of agricultural loans *	
With stations (N=550)**	Without stations (N=99)	With stations (n=8)	Without stations (n=6)
632 000 (Yuan)	211 000 (Yuan)	23.9 %	18.0 %

[a] "Rate of agricultural loans" means the proportion of farm households with farm production loans to the total number of farm households.

[b] "N" indicates the number of villages included in the group of townships .stations are much larger than in villages without credit stations. Considering that the average number of villages in a township without a village credit station amounts to only 3/5 of that for a township with a credit station, deposit scales were adjusted with 3/5 as the parameter. As a result, the per village average amount of deposits in townships with credit stations was RMB 379 thousand Yuan, still higher than the townships without stations. The reason for the greater amount of deposits is simply that there is a close correlation between the deposit amount and the village credit stations' convenient and swift monetary services. In comparison with this, there are many factors affecting the amount of loans, including the average income level of the villagers, township RCC-stipulated ceilings on total credit amounts and shares allocated to different sectors, situation of loan redemption in the past, credit of borrowers, etc., with the quality of financial services also being one of the important factors.

5. Behavior of Creditors and Debtors and Loan Repayment

The debtors in arrears to the ABCs are mainly the county enterprises, grain bureaus, cooperatives of supply and marketing and township enterprises. In the case of township Credit Cooperatives, the debtors include township enterprises, township governments, village committees and farm households, in decreasing order of the amounts for which the borrowers are in arrears. According to the survey of sampled township Credit Cooperatives, the loan repayment rate of township enterprises was only 47.3%, and the rate of delinquent loans (more than two years overdue and without any possibility of the loan being repaid) was as high as 31.4%. In the 34 townships sampled, three township governments obtained loans from rural Credit Cooperatives and repaid nothing. Of the village committees, 17 borrowed money from the Credit Cooperatives, and the repayment rate was 29%. The rate of loan recovery from farm households averaged 60%. Village credit stations generally grant loans only to individual households, and the rate of timely repayment averaged 58 percent. It is noteworthy that the lower the income of the households, the higher is the rate of loan repayment (Table 5.7). This fact is helpful in correcting a prevalent prejudice among the decision-makers of China's formal financial institutions, namely that the poorer farm households are, the lower is their rate of loan repayment.

In the rapid appraisal studies done in the context of this research, it was frequently mentioned that borrowers generally lacked credit ethics. More precisely, they did not apply normal repayment behavior to the formal credit institutions. In the field of informal loan business, the violation of a contract was very rare compared to those in the formal credit sector. In transactions with formal financial institutions, borrowers are not prevented from overextending themselves because there is a lack of effective credit restrictions. The change in the official rate of interest for loans usually lags behind increases in the inflation rate, and the sum of changes is less than the increase in inflation, so that the interest rate is actually negative. This situation is favorable for borrowers who take loans and pay in arrears. This is a direct financial incentive for borrowers to intentionally violate loan contracts.

As a response to the fictitious ownership of the bank, the borrowers think that the bank works on behalf of the state, and therefore 'take meals from a big pot of the state' and fail to keep the contract. All this seems to be a consequence of the planned economy which has not yet been overcome in rural financial systems. State and collective enterprises are the greatest borrowers in the countryside. The credit relationships between them and the formal credit institutions is just like a transaction from the "public" to the "public". The proprietors will protect their private assets, backed by the traditional relationship between individuals. However, the legal environment and the system for administering the social contract constrains the public sector to maintain its property. The managers of public enterprises are either officials appointed by the governments, or private contractors. Neither of them are held liable over the long term. If managers run an enterprise unsuccessfully, they will leave for other jobs or businesses without any personal losses, while the debt they incurred remains with the enterprise. Their successors will usually ignore the payments in arrears, or delay repayment of the loans under the pretext that it was the previous managers' fault. Eventually, the loss will be attributed to the bank. Moreover, the government officials who helped the enterprise to obtain the loans will exhibit similar, short-term conduct. The officials bear no further responsibility once they leave their positions.

Compared with enterprises, farmers (individuals) have much better credit consciousness. Local governments take care of industrial enterprises, but pay little or no heed to the investment potentials of individuals. Local governments often help enterprises to get loans, and even ask a favor for paying the debts in arrears because the operation of the enterprises affects the government's financial revenues and the target of employment provisions. Compared with enterprises, individual farm households clearly have little weight in the local economic and political power structure. The creditor-debtor relationship between financial institutions and farmers is easily identifiable. Farmers take small loans, mainly to supplement their working capital in production. In general, they borrow in spring and repay in summer, or borrow in summer and repay in autumn. However, if they take part in a project and get loans at a subsidized interest rate, they usually deem both the principal and the interest to be welfare given by the state. Based on such an understanding, farmers are often in arrears with payment and wait for their debts to be forgiven. In spite of the legal provisions, the laws are not strictly enough enforced, and even if the liabilities are investigated, the conventions that "the law will not punish the masses" also makes the violators unafraid and confident.

In addition, a number of farm households failed in implementing projects supported by local governments, such as those for developing specialized production, and then had the loans used to finance the projects forgiven. The farmers claimed that they had borrowed due to encouragement by the government, not to their own decisions. Because the concept derived from the planned economy, many farmers think that the state, government, and bank all belong to what is generally termed "the state". According to this logic, they reason that the liabilities are borne by the government, the debt should be paid by the state, and this is right and proper. As the philosophy of the market economy is gradually accepted, some farmers acknowledge debts, but are unable to repay them. There are a few cases in which individuals or whole families moved to another place of residence in order to avoid a debt, or to repudiate a debt in a mood of determination: "I have no money, but a life". In this case, the banks or Credit Cooperatives usually have to accept the loss because enforcement of the law is weak.

This description of the behavior of debtors shows that creditors can acquire only incomplete information on debtors' intentions and ability to repay. The creditors have to pay high costs to reduce the possibility of contract violation, to prompt debtors to keep their contracts, or to compel them to repay their loans. This is a common problem that exists in the rural credit sector all over the world (Hoff and Stiglitz, 1990). In China, the system of planned economy endowed special institutional, ideological and cultural features to credit institutions, industrial and commercial enterprises, and farm households. This made the problem more serious than in other countries. By the end of the 1980's, nearly all business organs of the Agriculture Bank and Rural Credit Cooperatives had large volumes of bad loans. The ABC branches and Credit Cooperatives adopted responses to this situation which were similar to those of credit institutions in a market economy:

1. Borrowers are required to provide collateral for loans exceeding certain amounts.
2. If borrowers cannot provide collateral, guarantees must be provided by third parties, secured through their assets.

3. Violators of contracts are punished through measures such as a higher rate of interest on the loan, increased rates of interest on future loans, prevention of future borrowing, etc. (Binswanger and Rosenzweig, 1986).

The agricultural banking system has meanwhile reformed its management based on the principles of "being self-responsible for profit or loss, and self-responsible for risks" (Division of Monetary Reforms, People's Bank of China, 1991). The aim of transforming the Agriculture Bank into a commercial bank was then clarified. Undoubtedly, these reforms intensified the relative independence of the bank's managerial decision-making and made its grass-roots officers pay more attention to the security of loans. At the grass-roots of rural society, the business coverage of the network of RCCs was originally denser and broader than that of the ABCs. After several serious failures occurred with loan provisions in the 1980s, the RCCs' managerial regulations were made stricter. The credit stations of the RCCs played an important role in monitoring loan use and ensuring loan recovery. Sooner or later, village credit officers succeed in collecting loans from the majority of farm households, except in very rare cases in which the borrowers were unable to pay or moved elsewhere to avoid having to repay the debts. In addition to their own service networks, some RCCs recover loans with the assistance of supply and marketing cooperatives and grain stations. For example, a farmer receives a credit card with a written loan amount in the sowing season and buys fertilizer with the credit card from the supply and marketing cooperative. The supply and marketing cooperative has a loan account in a Credit Cooperative, and it hands the credit card to the latter to clear the account. The farmer sells his products to the grain station after harvest. The station will subtract his loan with interest for the Credit Cooperative when it pays the farmer for his products. This measure effectively controls loan use and obviates the cash payment procedure. It seems to possess something of the operating style of modern financial institutions.

In view of the loan risks, all the ABCs and RCCs in the counties sampled are inclined to make short-term loans. Regarding the duration of the loans, those with a term of less than one year made up approximately 60%, of all loans while those with a term of one to three years amounted to about 30%. More than half of the rest fell into the category of three-to-five year loans, and there were very few loans with terms of more than 5 years. In developed countries, farmers receive medium and long-term loans, usually for ten to twenty years and sometimes with terms of even 30 years. The interest rates on medium- and long-term loans are generally lower than those for short-term loans (Zhu Ling, 1995b). Perhaps it is due to the bad reputation of the borrowers that China's rural credit institutions adopted the following interest-rate policy: the longer a loan's term, the higher its rate of interest. According to the information gathered from interviews with business officers of the ABCs and the RCCs, the risks and profits associated with different kinds of loans can be arranged in the order shown by Table 5.9. The capital letters A, B, C and D are used to indicate the ascending order of risks and profit associated with the loans from the ABCs and RCCs. To facilitate interpretation, only four kinds of loans are discussed in the following, i.e. agricultural short-term and medium-to-long-term loans, and industrial and commercial short-term and medium-to-long-term loans.

Table 5.9 Evaluations of Risks and Profit for Various Loans From Agriculture Bank Branches and Rural Credit Cooperatives in the Sampled Counties [a]

Loan category [b]	*Agriculture*		*Industry and commerce*	
	Short-term	Medium-long-term	Short term	Medium-long-term
Profit level	A [c]	A	C	D
Risk level	A	D	A	D

[a] evaluated based on researchers' interviews with credit officers from approx. 10 sample ABCs and RCCs. This is not an unique evaluation of the interview participants, but represents the views of approximately 80% of them.

[b] a simple classification: loans with terms of less than one year are deemed to be short-term loans, while those with longer terms are categorized as medium-to-long-term loans.

[c] The capital letters A through D are in ascending order.

Farmers would like to get loan with as low a rate of interest as possible in order to reduce their production costs. That is why many farmers use short-term loans in sequences and complete their investment projects in several steps, with each step being covered by a short-term loan. The RCCs also prefer to give priority to short-term loans for the sake of maintaining the security of their funds and their liquidity. For example, approximately 80% of the herdsmen of Inner Mongolian pastoral areas use short-term loans to make investments in well-drilling and fence construction even though these projects cannot be completed with the funds provided by the short-term loans. The herdsmen adopt the approach of "repay the loan and borrow again". The effect of a short-term loan is then close to that of a long-term loan. On average, each family needs 20,000 Yuan to construct fences, and most herdsmen divide their pastoral area into several pieces, and build their fences from piece to piece. This work will be completed in three to five years.

Each year, the loan will vary from 1,000 to 4,000 Yuan. To drill wells near their residence, they take the same approach of drilling deeper every year and then installing a pump and pipes. This usually takes from three to five years as well. In Laiyang County of Shandong province, farmers adopted the technique of sharing a large amount of short-term credit among several households in order to invest in the construction of a large vegetable shed. When the shed is completed, the debt will be distributed among the farmers according to the amount of space which each of them uses. The users will then pay their respective portions of the loan. However, choices between different kinds of loans may be limited by the nature of investment projects. For example, short-term loans are inappropriate for reclaiming hilly land or investing in forestry projects or orchards because the time required before forestry or orchards provide any return is long and the initial investment substantial. Farmers specializing in forest or fruit production therefore seem to use two kinds of loans: long-term loans for constructing infrastructure (digging channels, constructing roads and houses, obtaining a power supply, etc.), while sequences of short-term loans are used to plant trees and diversify side-line production. Many farmers who reclaimed the hilly land in Jiangxi Province adopted this means of implementing their investment plans. The above examples indicate that, because the system for managing social contracts is weak, both credit institutions and borrowers prefer short-term contracts. This may be seen as a rational response to the current economic and legal environment, but not as being favorable for capital investment with returns to scale, and hence must be considered to hinder rural development over the long run.

6. Some Conclusions

Formal financial institutions and their business networks have played an important role in mobilizing rural savings on a large scale and in financing industries and agriculture. During the transition from a planned to a market economy, the system of rural finance has been reformed, step by step, in the direction of more independent management. However, traces of the old system can still be seen everywhere in the operations of financial institutions, particularly in the fact that credit institutions are obliged to perform administratively assigned tasks and to implement state credit plans. Furthermore, credit institutions have not adopted the concepts and operating style of modern financial services. These institutions are still being run with a low degree of involvement in the economic activities of local enterprises, farms and households. It is therefore difficult to monitor loan use effectively. Rural credit institutions are troubled to various extents by problems of unsatisfactory security, profitability, and liquidity. At present, formal credit institutions in rural areas are confronted by two main difficulties: One is that credit institutions which are subject to direct interference from various levels of government lack the capacity to deal with risks. The other is that borrowers are unreliable in repaying loans because the system has not yet developed an effective mechanism for dissuading them from abrogating their contracts. These two institutional drawbacks could lead to serious credit crises. If a stability of a bank is not threatened by bad loans, the bank certainly omits controls on high-risk loans. If the system fails to develop strict measures for dealing with contract violators, borrowers will think it proper to take excessive risks to avoid repaying loans.

It is imperative to develop new legal bases regulating the rights and obligations of lenders and borrowers. This should include the establishment of inspection institutions, the supervision of bank operations, and the establishment of a system for insuring banks and deposits in order to secure the interests of depositors. Furthermore, it is necessary to set up a contract-management system which is capable of punishing contract violators.

Chapter Six

PARTICIPATION IN CREDIT SYSTEMS AND CREDIT UTILIZATION BY POOR HOUSEHOLDS

The ultimate aim of providing credit and savings services for the poor is to assist the poor in their efforts to overcome poverty. It should be illuminating to examine how the poor operate in rural China's present system of formal and informal finance, which elements of the system they utilize to meet their various financing needs and with what effect. This section presents insights obtained from household-level analyses. The presentation of the results below distinguishes between "poor households" and "non-poor households". For this purpose, the poverty line has been drawn at a household per capita income of 600 Yuan in 1993 (as in Chapter 5). In the sample, 30 percent of households fall below the poverty line defined in this way. There are 507 households with a per capita income between 600 and 1200 Yuan, while the rest (763 households) have a per capita income of more than 1200 Yuan. Comparative statistics of mean values of key variables such as income and consumption of major food items suggest that the sample comes close to an average of the poor regions of rural China in the early 1990s.

1. Distribution of Poor Households Among the Sample Villages

1.1. The village situation: a cluster analysis

To describe the socioeconomic environment in which the poor households exist, a cluster analysis was performed on 34 sample villages. The following six variables were used as cluster indices:

1. per capita income;
2. share of agricultural labor (proportion of labor force in farm production relative to total labor force of village);
3. share of agricultural capital (proportion of agricultural fixed assets to total assets of village);
4. yields (food grain output per mu);
5. agricultural sector share (proportion of gross value of farm production to that of total production of village);
6. education (proportion of illiterate labor to total labor force of village).

This cluster analysis led to the villages being classified into four groups with different levels of economic and social development. The four groups into which the 34 sample villages were divided through the cluster analysis are shown in Table 6.1. Differences in the economic structures of the four categories of villages (Table 6.2) recapitulate the development process of rural villages from underdeveloped agricultural villages to villages which have achieved initial industrialization.

Table 6.1 Results of Cluster Analysis of Sample Villages

Low-income group	Medium-low-income group	Medium-high-income group	High-income group
Xiaozhai village of Shanxi's Pingshun county	Lijiajiao village of Shanxi's Liulin	Xiangyang village of inner-Mongolia's (Neimeng's) Linhe	Xishufu village of Zhejiang's Shaoxing
Zugang village of Henan's Xincai county	Doujing village of Shanxi's Linyi	Daijia village of inner-Mongolia's Tongliao	Miaoyan village of Zhejiang's Yinxian
Changhe village of Sichuan's Fengjie county	Longzhou village of Jiangxi's Taihe	Qiaoxia village of Jiangxi's Shangrao	Muyun'an village of Shandong's Rongcheng
Yunshan village of Yunnan's Lancang	Mingzha village of Jiangxi's Jiujiang	Liugou village of Shandong's Laiyang	
Yuanyang village of Yunnan's Huize	Shiguan village of Henan's Anyang	Xiayuan village of Gansu's Wuwei	
Fangshu village of Yunnan's Wuding	Dasiguo village of Henan's Taiquian	Pingling village of Jilin's Lishu	
Chenma village of Gansu's Huining	Yuejin village of Sichuan's Jiange	Paibangshu village of Guangxi's Yulin	
Moshan village of Gansu's Linxia	Lianhe village of Sichuan's Gulin		
Da'an village of Jilin's Minqiang	Xinfeng village of Jilin's Tongyu		
Sanliu village of Shaanxi's Hanyin	Pingshan village of Guangxi's Longan		
	Pingman village of Guangxi's Tianlin		
	Ciyu village of Shaaxi's Pucheng		
	Xifurao village of Shaanxi's Zhouzhi		

Table 6.2 Comparison of the Economic Structures of the 4 Village Groups, 1993

Group of village	Full-time farmers' households /total households of a village (%)	Number of collective and joint-stock enterprises per village	Labor force in farm production /total labor force (%)	Per capita farm land (mu)	Average food grain output per mu (kg)	Per capita net income (Yuan)
I Poorest (n=10)	72.0	0.20	60.3	2.86	159	419
II (n=14)	46.7	1.86	52.2	1.90	280	1006
III (n=7)	41.5	2.00	31.4	1.64	445	1121
IV Richest (n=3)	13.5	9.00	3.0	0.53	354	2645

Table 6.3 Agro-Economic Development and Market Integration of Staple Farm Products in the 4 Village Groups, 1993

Village groups	Average per capita area of farm land (mu)	Average food grain output per mu (kg)	Ratio of food grain output to area of farm land / total area	Rate of food grain marketing	Rate of pork marketing	Rate of poultry marketing
Poorest I	2.86	159	0.83	0.053	0.49	0.45
II	1.90	280	0.78	0.068	0.72	0.36
III	1.64	445	0.81	0.065	0.71	0.36
Richest IV	0.53	354	0.89	0.003	1.00	0.19

In the course of development, the proportion of full-time farming households and of the labor force in farm production decreased continuously, while village-operated collectives and joint-stock enterprises increased. Villages with a higher degree of industrialization also have higher population densities, which is reflected in a higher person-to-land ratio than that in less industrialized villages. Although the per capita area of farm land in the villages of the fourth group is only 1/5 of that in the first group, they are all located on the plains of east China's coastal regions, where not only the land quality but also the agro-climate is much better than in the first group of villages. The average food grain output per unit area (mu) in the fourth group of villages is therefore much higher than that in the villages of the first group.

The trend of *social development* in the villages of the four groups generally coincides with their *economic development* (Tables 6.3 and 6.4), and improved economic development is also revealed in better services (including credit service). However, poor people exist not only in poor villages: of the 650 poor households with a per capita income below 600 Yuan, 457 were located in the ten poor villages of group I, while the rest (around 30 percent of the poor households in the sample) were distributed among the other groups. This implies that anti-poverty measures should be extended to individual poor households in non-poor areas since a considerable share of poor people fall into this low-income group. The average per capita income of villages in group I was 419 Yuan per annum (Table 6.5), i.e. below the poverty line of 700 Yuan, so that these villages can be regarded as poor villages. The structure of income sources shows that their farm-production and animal-husbandry incomes were the highest of all, which was typical of the poor villages where traditional farming with comparatively low productivity remains the mainstay of the economy. Per capita incomes in the villages of groups II and III were approaching the 1993 national average level of 1120 Yuan. Their higher income level was due mainly to their industrial development.

Table 6.4 Social Development Levels of the 4 Village Groups, 1993

Village groups	TV sets per household	Proportion of labor with more than 9 year's schooling (%)	Proportion of households with running water (%)	Proportion of households with electricity (%)	Infant mortality (%)
Poorest I	0.11	3	41	26	5
II	0.57	10	74	94	5
III	0.62	7	25	99	2
Richest IV	0.92	12	97	100	0

Table 6.5 Income Structure of the 4 Village Groups, 1993

Index / village group	Per capita income (RMB Yuan)	Farm-production income /total income	Animal-breeding income / total income	Industrial income / total income	Construction income / total income	Transportation income /total income
I	419	0.53	0.23	0.02	0.00	0.03
II	1006	0.24	0.10	0.50	0.02	0.03
III	1121	0.22	0.10	0.42	0.11	0.04
IV	2645	0.01	0.01	0.81	0.03	0.01

Due to the limited availability of farmland, the development of rural enterprises had become the chief means of achieving comparatively rapid increases in income. The agricultural income of the villages in group IV accounted for only 1% of their total income, indicating that this category of villages has realized industrialization. The collective economies in group I villages were negligible (Table 6.6). Due to the fact that the funds turned over by farm households were insufficient to support the villages' normal expenses, the villages had to rely on subsidies from higher-level governments or on borrowing.

Table 6.6 Financial Situation of the 4 Village Groups, 1993

	Collective income / total income	Ratio of farm income / total income	Collective investment / total expenditure	Production services expenditure / total expenditure	Deposit balance / total households (Yuan)	Credit balance / total households (Yuan)	Collective debts to individual households / total households
I Poorest	0.02	0.23	0.00	0.04	16	6	16
II	0.22	0.28	0.06	0.33	36	18	10
III	0.71	0.23	0.39	0.20	62	77	14
IV Richest	0.98	0.01	0.98	0.00	314	6169	0

1.2. Role of credit for different types of villages

With the development of industrialization, the villages' collective economies have become more active, and their production investments increased continuously. Because farming was still the main economic activity of the villages, their investments in the agriculture support system was also growing, which was an important factor boosting the agricultural development in the group II and III villages. The levels of village collectives' per household debt in different villages (last column of Table 6.6) differs a great deal between poor and relatively rich villages. Villages with higher levels of economic development can obtain more loans, while villages with lower levels of development had difficulties securing loans from ABC county branches (or RCCs).

To identify the relationship between participation in credit markets and the characteristics of poor villages, we divide the poorest villages of group I into two further subgroups, i.e. those *with formal financial services* and those *without* (Table 6.7). Poor villages *with* financial services had a better-qualified labor force (column 6, Table 6.7). They also had a higher proportion of collectively-owned assets than villages without utilisation of credit. In addition, the villages with financial services spent more money for agricultural services (column 3, Table 6.7) than those without financial services. Although the food grain yields of the former exceeded those of the latter by only a small margin, it is noteworthy that villages with credit support show more favorable conditions. Here, there is probably a causal link in both directions: a better human-resource base may have facilitated accelerated investment, and availability of credit may have facilitated investment, which might in turn have increased demand for better education. In any case, access to financing is part of promising developments even among the poorest villages.

Table 6.7 Characteristics of *Poor Villages* with and without Formal Financial Services 1993

	Number of poor sample villages	Farm-production labor force / village total labor force	Collective assets / village total assets	Agro-service expenditures / village total expenditure	Food grain output per mu (kg)	Illiterate labor force /total labor force
With fin. services	3	0.78	0.20	0.10	200	0.19
Without fin. services	7	0.74	0.09	0.04	197	0.42

2. Credit in Poor Households in Poor Rural Villages

Poor villages include some people with participation in credit markets and some without. In the ten poor villages of group I, there were 457 poor farm households (per capita incomes below RMB 600 Yuan), which amounts to 24% of all households. Of these, 55 households had *established credit relations with the township* RCC (constituting 12% of the total poor households). We were curious to see in what way these *poor households in poor villages* with participation in credit markets differed from those without participation. To gain insight into the impact of credit support on the improvement of poor households' economic conditions, we made some comparisons. First, we found that poor farmer households' loans from ABC branches (or RCCs) accounted for 70% of all their debts. Table 6.8 shows the situation of loans given to poor households in poor villages. The households without formal credit (a negligible 14 Yuan) utilized some credit from informal sources, especially for consumption purposes.[5]

Table 6.8 Utilization of Credit by Poor Households in Poor Rural Villages (RMB/household in 1993)

Item / group	Total borrowings	RCC loans	Loans for living expenses	Loans for production	Agricultural loans
With loans	485	338	194	291	145
Without loans	145	14	88	56	34

[5] It is necessary to clarify here that low-interest loans given directly to poor farm households accounted for only about 30 % of poverty-reduction loans, while the remainder had gone to rural enterprises and related units conducting poverty-reduction projects.

Table 6.9 Farm-Production Expenses of Poor Households in Poor Rural Villages (RMB/household in 1993)

Item / group	Seed expenditure	Diesel oil expenditure	Amount of fertilizers bought (kg)	Plastic film expenditure	Total farm-production inputs
With loans	43.9	14.8	267	5.7	264.5
Without loans	20.0	8.6	250	5.8	229.8

Table 6.10 Income of Poor Households in Poor Rural Villages (RMB/household in 1993)

Item / group	Gross income	Production expenses	Cash income / total income (%)	Food-grain and cash-crop incomes	Net income	Service income / total income
With loans	3.330	1.324	40	1.397	2.006	25.8
Without loans	2.729	1.045	40	1.335	1.533	27.0

Table 6.11 Consumption Expenditures of Poor Households in Poor Rural Villages (RMB/household in 1993)

Item / group	Total living expenditure	Food	Clothes	Fuel	Daily necessities	Services	Per capita total
With loans	2.302	1.454	150	172	157	75	456
Without loans	1.905	1.274	155	105	133	69	404

The production facilities of households with participation in credit markets were slightly superior to those of households without participation. Livestock assets were also slightly greater in the group with participation. The former's total input of production expenditures was also higher than the latter's, but the difference in their incomes was mainly physical, rather than cash (Table 6.9). Both the gross incomes and net incomes of households with participation to credit were higher than those of the group without participation (Table 6.10). Most of the consumption expenditures of the households with participation to formal credit were higher than those of the other group (Table 6.11). Households in the first group consumed more food of four main items than those in the other group, as shown in Table 6.12. In general, the food consumption level of poor households with participation in credit markets was higher than that of the poor group without participation.

Table 6.12 Food Consumption of Poor Households in Poor Rural Villages (kg/household in 1993)

Item / group	Food-grain consumption	Edible oil consumption	Poultry consumption	Vegetable consumption	Pork consumption	Egg consumption
With loans	1.150	7.7	3.2	320	68	4.8
Without loans	1.082	6.8	4	382	58	4.5

The comparative analyses in the above tables suggest that participation in credit markets had reinforced poor farmers' use of inputs, increased their incomes, and improved their level of food consumption.

3. Participation in Credit Systems and Patterns of Utilization

The patterns and determinants of participation in credit markets at a household level are analyzed further below. In contrast to the tables above, this analysis considers *all sources of credit* and places special emphasis on informal sources of credit, which seem to be of particular relevance for the poor.

Loans may be divided into four different categories:

- loans from banks (all formal institutions, including Credit Cooperatives);
- loans from private sources, with interest payments;
- loans from private sources, without interest payments and
- other loans.

3.1. Loan sources and patterns of utilization

We first asked

- whether poor households have participated less in credit markets (determined simply by the ratio of households which have obtained loans in the previous year) compared to non-poor households, and
- for which purposes the poor use the loans.

Our findings can be summarized as follows:

1. A larger ratio of the poor households obtained a loan than did the non-poor households: 31% of poor households as compared to 27% of non-poor ones (see Figures 6.1 and 6.2).
2. In general, the pattern of loan sources does not differ much between poor and non-poor households. Poor households take a slightly lower percentage from banks (29%) than non-poor households (32%). In both groups, private loans without interest are the most frequently utilized source of loans (48% and 45%, respectively, see Figures 6.1 and 6.2).
3. Clearly, *private sources of loans are very important for financing in poor areas of China*. Households which actually took loans

took quite significant ones, compared to their present annual income.

4. Bank loans (also smaller than loans from private sources, as well as private loans with interest-rate payments) are actually much more relevant (measured relative to income) among poor households than among non-poor households (in case of bank loans, for example, 42% versus 28% for the two groups, respectively, see Figures 6.1 and 6.2).

Figure 6.1 Loan Structure and Use Pattern Among Poor Households

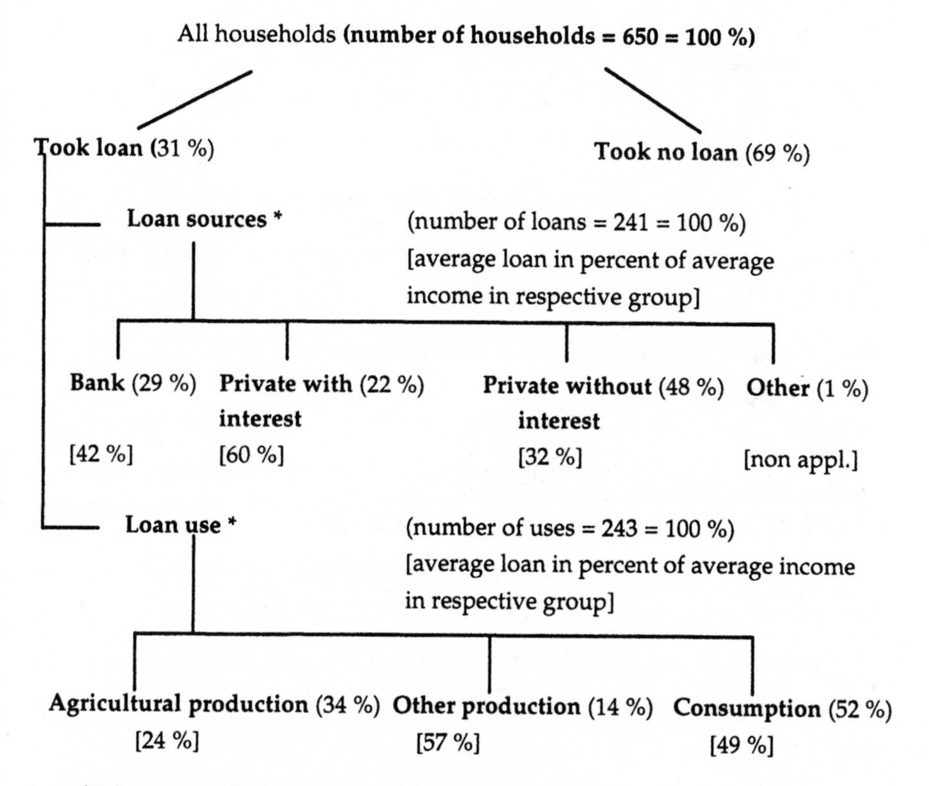

*: multiple responses for loan source and loan use were allowed

Figure 6.2 Loan Structure and Use Pattern Among Non-Poor Households

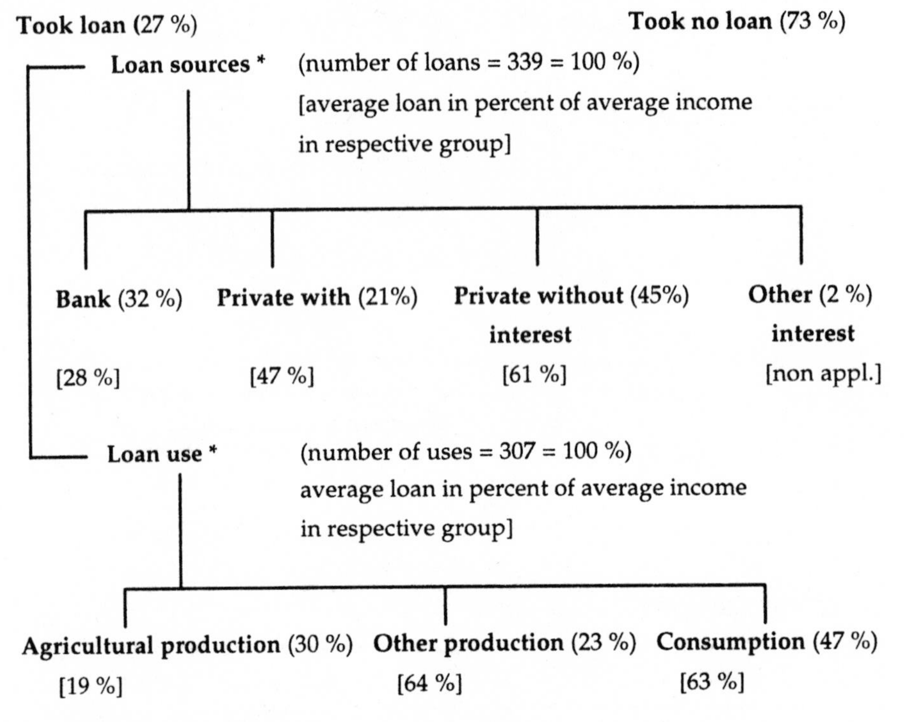

* : multiple responses for loan source and loan use were allowed

3.2. Important role of consumer credit

The mean per capita loan value was 179 Yuan in the poor group, and 807 in the non-poor group (see the bottom of column 3, Tables 6.13 A and B). Given the difference in income between these two groups (362 versus 1273 Yuan per capita), this suggests a nearly *linear increase of per capita consumer loans as per capita income rises.* The patterns of loan use highlight the important role of consumer credit for the poor. Of the poor households which actually took a loan, 52% report that they used it for consumption purposes, while agriculture predominated among production purposes, accounting for 34% (see Figure 6.1). Both figures are relatively lower for the non-poor households group (see Figure 6.2). Consumer loans matter not only in terms of their frequency, but also in terms of their amount relative to annual income. In the group which actually took consumer loans, these loans represented 49% of the income of the poor household group.

The statistics on loan-source and loan-use patterns also take into account multiple responses regarding loan sources and uses and indicate a rather limited scale of broad-based fungibility of funds (see Tables 6.13 A,B,C). For example, the total number of consumer loans taken out by the 650 households in the poor household's group adds up to 153. The number of households which actually state that they took some consumer loan was 126. Thus, the number of multiple sources used for different consumer loans is not much larger than the number of households stating that they took any consumer loan, that is 126 (see column 3, Table 6.13 a).

Both poor households and non-poor households take *private loans without interest* in combination with bank loans (see Tables 6.13 A and B) to a significant extent. Also, poor households which took consumer loans to a substantial extent, also borrowed for agricultural investments at the same time (29 of 126 consumer loan takers, as shown in Table 6.13 c).

Interesting, too, are the two groups' patterns of use of *loans obtained from banks*: poor households use about half of bank loans for consumption purposes, whereas the non-poor households use a smaller fraction for these purposes. (Note again that adding up all bank loans per use pattern includes overlapping several loans to some extent.). It is also important to note that *private loans without interest are utilized for agricultural production* purposes to a substantial extent, and much more so among poor households, (see Table 6.13 A, first column, 4th row). The private self-help system is thus central to agricultural investment financing by the poor at the present time.

Table 6.13 a Loan *Sources* and Loan *Use* Among Poor Households)

	Agricultural loan	Other productive loan	Consumer loan	Total n*	mean income/ cap.	mean loan/ cap.
No loan	—	—	—	450	414	—
Bank loan	41	14	34	69	393	165
Private loan with interest	7	17	41	54	320	193
Private loan without interest	58	15	75	115	408	132
Other loan	1	—	3	3	382	807
Total n*	83	34	126	650		
mean income/cap.	422	364	362			
mean loan/cap.	100	208	179			

Table 6.13 b Using Loans from Multiple *Sources* (poor households)

	Bank loan	Private loan with interest	Private loan without interest	Other loan	Total n*
Bank loan	***				69
Private loan with interest	13	***			54
Private loan without interest	24	3	***		115
Other loan	2	—	1	***	3

Table 6.13 c Using of Loans for Multiple *Purposes* (poor households)

	Agricultural loan	Other productive loan	Consumer loan	Total n*
Agricultural loan	***			83
Other productive loan	2	***		34
Consumer loan	29	13	***	126

* : The individual observation tallies do not add up to Total n because of multiple responses

Table 6.14 a Loan *Sources* and Loan *Use* (non-poor households)

	Agricultural loan	Other productive loan	Consumer loan	Total n*	mean income /cap.	mean loan/cap.
No loan	—	—	—	992	1498	—
Bank loan	53	34	38	107	1138	322
Private loan with interest	14	13	53	72	1178	555
Private loan without interest	52	38	80	152	1199	727
Other loan	4	4	5	8	1089	1535
Total n*	92	72	143	1270		
mean income/cap.	944	1235	1273			
mean loan/cap.	177	785	807			

Table 6.14 b Using Loans from Multiple *Sources* (non-poor households)

	Bank loan	Private loan with interest	Private loan without interest	Other loan	Total n*
Bank loan	***				107
Private loan with interest	17	***			152
Private loan without interest	34	7	***		72
other loan	4	2	2	***	8

Table 6.14 c Using Loans for Multiple *Purposes* (non-poor households)

	Agricultural loan	Other productive loan	Consumer loan	Total n*
Agricultural loan	***			92
Other productive loan	5	***		72
Consumer loan	16	10	***	143

* : The individual observation tallies do not add up to Total n because of multiple responses

4. Analysis of Participation in Credit Systems and its Impact on Food Consumption

As described above, households in rural areas utilize to a certain degree formal banking institutions of different kinds, but make greater use of their possibilities of borrowing from private sources, especially from family and friends. The econometric analysis below addressed the following questions:

- What determines participation in formal credit systems on the one hand, and utilisation of credit from private sources on the other hand?

- What are the determinants of the size of such loans? This was assessed for the households which actually obtained credit from formal or informal sources.
- What is the impact on consumption of loans from formal versus loans from informal sources?[6]

4.1. Determinants of Participation in Credit Systems

Anyone who has obtained a loan from a *formal source* may obviously be considered to have participated in the formal segment of the credit system in the year under observation (1993). Similarly, households which have obtained loans from *informal and private sources may be* considered to have participated in that sector of the rural finance system. We hypothesize that participation in the credit system is determined by a set of

- institutional and infrastructure-related factors (e.g. level of rural finance activities in the province and distance from the village to the next county center),
- household-level economic factors representing the asset base (deposits and other assets held by the household, size of farm) and
- human-resource-related variables (education, age of household head and household size).

---

[6] While the data set described above offers opportunities to address all these questions to some extent, it is necessary to bear in mind certain limitations which prevent a fully satisfactory analytical approach. This applies in particular to the drawing of a destinction between the possibilities of access involving more specific separation of the determinants of willingness to borrow and the constraints on borrowing (Jappelli, T. 1990; Zeller, M. et.al.1996). A comprehensive analysis of the frequency and consequences of being subject to credit constraints cannot be performed in this context. The analysis is therefore largely confined to the determinants and effects of participation in credit systems.

For the participation in the informal credit system, the penetration of formal banking activities into the province may also have an impact on informal lending activities. We therefore assume that participation in private lending is determined partly by the level of formal banking activities in the relevant province.

Here, we employ a uni-variate probit approach in which we determine the probability of participation in each sector (formal and informal):

(1) *Probability of participation = f(institutional environment, infrastructure environment; asset base of household; human-resource situation of household),*

where 'participation' is a (0,1) dummy variable which is '1' if the household obtained some credit and '0' otherwise. The results of the probit estimates are listed in Table 6.15. Our analysis shows that institutional-level factors, especially the level of banking activity in

Table 6.15 a Determinants of Participation in Credit Systems

a. Formal Credit Sector (Estimation results of PROBIT model)

Regression Coeff.		t-values
HOUSIZE	0.0355	1.48
ASSETS	-0.00001	-0.85
LAND	0.0058	0.34
DISTANCE	-0.0204	-1.12
EDUCAT	0.0535	0.97
AGEHEAD	0.0096	0.22
PROVBANK	0.6814	6.88
Intercept		
	-2,004	-8,078

n = 1,797

b. Informal Credit Sector (Results of PROBIT model estimates)

Regression Coeff.		t-values
HOUSIZE	0.0418	2.11
ASSETS	-0.00001	-1.03
LAND	-0.0403	-2.46
DISTANCE	0.0157	1.04
EDUCAT	-0.0743	-1.68
AGEHEAD	-0.0750	-2.18
PROVBANK	0.1661	2.31
Intercept		
	-0.635	-3.25

n = 1,797

Description of variables (mean values of variables in (..)):

HOUSIZE (4.59) = household size (persons)

ASSETS (2403.37) = household assets and deposits per capita (in Yuan)

LAND (2.38) = per capita land area in mu

DISTANCE (1.85) = distance of village from road (in km)

EDUCAT (2.28) = education level of household's main income earner (grade achieved)

AGEHEAD (2.69) = age of head of household (age groups, 1= 20-30, 2=30-40 etc.)

PROVBANK (0.55) = intensity of banking in the province (= 1 if more than 10% of households obtained credit; 0 otherwise)

the province, and infrastructure are significant determinants of participation in the *formal sector*. Household-level economic factors including human-resource factors seem to play only a limited role in determining participation or nonparticipation.

In the case of utilisation of loans from *private sources*, our analysis indicates first that the penetration of financial services in the province seems to have a favorable effect on the probability of obtaining loans from private sources in the same province, i.e. wherever the formal sector is more active, the private and informal sector also seems to be stimulated, with the effect of improving participation. The two sectors seem to move together to some extent. It is also interesting to note that younger households with low levels of education are participating more actively in the private lending system. This may be due to a lack of alternatives. Education played no role (i.e. was found statistically non-significant) in determining participation in the credit system.

4.2. Determinants of volume of credit at household level

Once a loan becomes obtainable, its size is determined endogenously by prices (interest, transactions costs), loan securities (assets), and desired investment (scale economies and expected returns) and/or consumption objectives. We employ the Heckmann procedure for estimates of the quantitative impact of some of these determinants as identified in model (1) already (including the Mills Ratio).*(2) Predicted participation = f(institutional environment, infrastructure environment; asset base of household; human-resource situation of household)*

Although desirable, interest rate and transaction cost factors cannot be included properly, however, due to data constraints. The results of the regression analysis are presented in Table 6.16, both for the formal and the informal private loan determination (where Lambda represents the Mills Ratio).

Table 6.16 Determinats of Size of Loans Obtained by Households

a. Formal Sector

Variable	B	Beta	T
HOUSIZE	18.446	0.06	0.97
ASSETS	0.111	0.54	8.33
LAND	-14.321	-0.08	-1.31
DISTANCE	-4.767	-0.02	-0.37
EDUCAT	6.056	0.01	0.14
AGEHEAD	-12.493	-0.24	-0.38
LAMBDA	525.893	0.25	3.69
(Constant)	-841.497		

Adjusted R Square: 0.388

F = 16.82

No. of observations: 176

b. Informal Sources

Variable	B	Beta	T
HOUSIZE	-981.867	-1.21	-1.83
ASSETS	0.478	1.51	3.48
LAND	944.667	1.39	1.78
DISTANCE	-358.964	-0.64	-1.76
EDUCAT	1684.832	1.09	1.75
AGEHEAD	1635.377	1.30	1.67
BANKPROV	-3823.6	-1.40	-1.78
LAMBDA	-29744	-2.94	-1.77
(Constant)	37238.9		1.79

Adjusted R Square: 0.577

F = 65.88

No. of observations: 382

For description of independent variables (mean values of variables in (..)): see Table 6.15 dependent variables:

FORMAL (260.34) = predicted amount of formal credit (in yuan).

INFORMAL (460.32) = predicted amount of informal credit (in yuan)

The size of the loans obtained appears to be determined to a large extent by the *assets and deposits* of the household. This is actually the only highly significant variable in the models explaining size of loans for the subsample of those households which actually got loans (Table 6.16 A, B). The size of the asset base is of similar significance for the amount of formal and informal loans, and in the private informal sector is actually even more significant. The case studies conducted in Yunnan Province in 1996 also showed that the poorest had neither access to formal credit, nor they had possibilities to obtain private loans (Zhu Ling, 1996). This strongly underscores the conclusion that asset-poor households are largely excluded from participation in credit systems.

Additional analysis not presented suggest that, of the different types of property, it is mainly the household's monetary deposits which are significantly correlated with the size of loan obtained (correlation coefficient = .53). The greater the deposits a household has made in the RCCs, the larger the loans it borrowed (or was allowed to borrow) from the institutions. RCCs apparently take the monetary deposits of the borrowers' households as their principal credit guarantees. This is consistent with the information collected in interviews with RCC credit officers.

Given the nature of *land ownership* and land markets in China, it is not surprising that the size of farms does not seem to influence the size of loans (since it was not permitted to trade land in the market and farmers have only usufruct rights on farm land, while the land itself belongs to the village communities). At present, even though land has become legally tradable, the RCCs are reluctant to accept it as security for loans because farmers in the village would hardly like to buy his/her neighbors' land under circumstances when someone known to them may have fallen into such an awkward predicament due to problems with loan repayment. Furthermore, the market for other assets in rural areas, especially in poor regions, is not well developed. RCCs therefore prefer monetary deposits as guarantees for the provision of loans.

4.3. Impact of Credit on Consumption

Lastly, we trace the impact of credit both from the formal and the informal sectors on the consumption of food. For this purpose, we linked to the above econometric analysis the overall food expenditures (including value of home-produced food). The theoretical concept is that participation in credit systems, being determined partly by the complex set of non-household factors (institutional and infrastructure factors), has an impact on consumption over and above the standard set of consumption determinants (income, prices, etc.). The hypothesis to be explored is that participation in credit systems expands household consumption options because liquidity constraints are less severe under conditions of more active financial systems.

In the *model of food consumption expenditures,* we also include the predicted utilizations of formal and informal loans, respectively, as estimated in model 2 above. By including the credit utilizations as predicted in model 2, we test the effect of household's credit utilization on food expenditures (which is the effect over and above income):3) *food consumption expenditures = f(per capita income, household demographics, prices of staple foods, predicted utilization of formal and informal credit) (3)*

The results of the regression analysis are presented in Table 6.17 for the whole sample, as well as separately for the households classified as poor across provinces.

Table 6.17 Food Consumption Expenditures and Credit

a. All households

Variable	B	Beta	T
INCOME	0.141	0.61	34.35
HOUSIZE	-17.817	-0.09	-5.43
WHEATPRICE	678.112	0.11	6.22
RICEPRICE	-1009.895	-0.17	-9.76
BANKPRED	-0.022	-0.01	-0.49
PRIVPRED	0.022	0.34	1.90
(Constant)	544.511		5.46

Adjusted R Square: 0.496

F = 295.17

No of observations: 1.796

Description of variables (mean values of variables in (..)):

dependent: = food expenditure (415.85) in Yuan per capita

INCOME (1037.02) = per capita income in Yuan

HOUSIZE (4.60) = household size

WHEATPRICE (0.75) = wheat price in the county in Yuan per kilogram

RICEPRICE (0.70) = rice price in the county in Yuan per kilogram

BANKPRED (25.51) = predicted bank loans per capita in Yuan (from model 2a above)

PRIVPRED (97.91) = predicted private loans per capita in Yuan (from model 2b above)

b. Poor households

Variable	B	Beta	T
INCOME	0.291	0.33	8.88
HOUSIZE	-9.343	-0.15	-4.12
WHEATPRICE	-60.543	-0.03	-0.72
RICEPRICE	-368.781	-0.18	-4.52
BANKPRED	0.025	0.02	0.54
PRIVPRED	0.033	0.04	1.17
(Constant)	487.250		6.97

Adjusted R Square: 0.147

F = 19.45

No of observations: 643

Description of variables (mean values of variables in (..)):dependent: = food expenditure (262.33) in Yuan per capita

INCOME (406.16) = per capita income in Yuan

HOUSIZE (4.82) = household size

WHEATPRICE (0.74) = wheat price in the county in Yuan per kilogram

RICEPRICE (0.69) = rice price in the county in Yuan per kilogram

BANKPRED (21.77) = predicted bank loans per capita in Yuan (from model 2a above)

PRIVPRED (48.45) = predicted private loans per capita in Yuan (from model 2b above)

As typically expected, increased income significantly raises food consumption, and particularly among the poor, where from an additional Yuan .29 Yuan are spend on food. The estimation results also suggest that participation in credit systems of the informal sector, tends to raise consumption expenditures over and above the income effect of having access to credit, which is captured by the variables INCOME and PRIVPRED, respectively. The statistics of significance tests for PRIVPRED are, however, not particularly strong in either case. More detailed seasonal information is probably needed to properly test for consumption effects of credit utilisation.

5. Some Conclusions

It is evident that *informal* lending is already very active in rural China, exceeding the lending operations from formal bank sources. It is also important to stress that there is wide-spread utilization of credit for consumption. This should not be considered an 'unproductive' use of financial resources since the poor use such resources for human-resource maintenance and improvement, including the consumption of required staple foods. In contrast to what is often expected, loans from *formal* institutions are also utilized to a substantial extent for consumption purposes. Among the rural poor, however, loans from formal sources (banks) are used largely for farm production purposes. Expanding the rural finance system in poor areas will be particularly beneficial to the poor and to economic development and human-resource improvement in poor areas. The opportunity of participation in credit systems facilitates welfare even in the poorest villages and in the poor households there, as is suggested by comparative analyses of villages and poor households with and without participation in credit systems.

Chapter Seven

POLICY CONCLUSIONS

1. CREDIT SYSTEM CHANGES AS PART OF ECONOMIC REFORMS

1) As an essential element of China's economic reform, its markets for products, services and labor have become more open and flexible. However, this market orientation has not yet reached far into the important markets for credit and finance, especially in rural areas. The *need to activate financial markets* and related services is particularly relevant *in the poor rural areas* in order to facilitate these areas' participation in the process of economic growth and development which is proceeding much more rapidly in other regions of the country.

2) The credit-systems development and its poverty aspects ,in particular, must be seen in their relationship to *labor markets* and the opportunities of credit stimulating self-employment of the poor in the small-business sector. Furthermore, credit-system development for the poor is to be viewed in relation to insurance problems faced by the poor in a market economy.

3) The less flexibly financial systems respond, the stronger will be the adjustment pressures on the labor market. This means that, if capital cannot move freely and at low transactions costs to investment opportunities in poor rural areas, *labor movements* will be accelerated, and the cost of integrating the poor areas in the economic development process will increase in the future. There are investment opportunities in a scattered form in poor rural areas, largely related to small-scale farming, agricultural processing and village enterprises, all of which have considerable needs for financing needs and are labor-intensive.

2. Addressing Existing Problems in Rural Finance

4) The officially fixed, low *interest rates* have led the banks to exclude a huge number of small customers from the programs for the sake of keeping transaction costs down. The large amount of subsidies involved in the credit programs not only induced various interest-seeking activities, but also left different levels of government opportunities to interfere directly in the credit business of the banks. *Administrative interference gradually redirected the programs away from the initial target groups.* At the same time, credit risks increased as the responsibility for loans became unclear.

5) The *poorest segments of the population are often not integrated directly into the programs*; constraints on women's participation in development are not adequately addressed; poverty problems in non-poor areas have drawn but little public attention. It is therefore necessary to rethink the poverty-reduction strategies and to modify the financial-assistance programs for the coming decades.

6) The rural banking system does not cater appropriately to the market demand and the needs of the poor. This is highlighted by two characteristics found in the household-level analysis: (1) widespread borrowing from family and friends by the poor because they lack opportunities to use the formal system. Many good, small-scale investments may never be realized due to a lack of relations to the informal private supply of credit. (2) The poor's widespread use of credit to meet consumer needs (food-security needs, medical needs) is not being responded to by the formal sector, and so again leads to a great deal of borrowing from the private sector, including family and friends.

7) Comprehensive *adjustments to the rural financial system are yet to be considered* and designed. They will have to take the specific constraints, needs and potentials of the rural poor into account in the establishment of financial systems. There seems a lot of opportunity and scope for further experimentation with changes to the financial system ,especially in poor rural areas where poor households rely largely on family and friends to cope with credit needs. Today's *poor* should not be seen as recipients, but *as active partners* in the development of new financial institutions.

3. Poverty Reduction Through Credit: From Regional to Individual Targeting and Self-Help

8) During the past decade, China has achieved notable progress in reducing absolute poverty. Market-oriented reforms and resulting economic growth were instrumental in this, along with public policy for targeted poverty reduction. Such targeting focused to a large extent on poor areas (not households) with agriculture and infrastructure investments, employment programs, and transfers.

9) Regional development programs for poor areas should be differentiated from poverty-reduction programs. The absolute poor are still concentrated in poor areas, partly as a result of policies which have forbidden the free mobility of production factors (incl. labor) under the planned economy, but poor people are not equivalent to poor areas.

10) It is assumed here that the *broad outlines of China's poverty-reduction strategy will* be: (1) the central government will continue to provide development assistance to poor counties through regional targeting mechanisms in order to keep the nation unified by reducing regional differences. Under the circumstances, it would not be possible to completely exclude the non-poor in such regions from the range of beneficiaries. (2) The central government will also adopt mechanisms to assist the poorest people individually in order to maintain social stability by meeting the basic needs of these low-income groups. This approach is taken by the "National Anti-Poverty Plan for the Years of 1994-2000" (Chen Junsheng, 1994). Based on this basic understanding, the average poor groups shall benefit by both regional development and poverty-reduction programs and are sustainably assisted to rise above the poverty line, primarily through local economic growth and self-help measures. Later on, public assistance could be limited to the poorest groups.

11) It is important to note that, during the transition to a market economy, poverty issues in China are no longer simply regional problems and no longer confined to the rural sector. Paralleling the introduction of market functions, the unemployment concealed by the planned economy is becoming an increasingly visible problem. Large numbers of jobs will be lost in unproductive former public

enterprises, and many who loose their employment may fall into poverty unless measures are taken to prevent it. In response to this changing situation, it is necessary to adopt *individual targeting approaches rather than area targeting* in the implementation of effective and efficient poverty-reduction programs.

12) The regional development programs are helpful in reducing poverty because the regional deficiencies (e.g. infrastructure) have significant effects on income. In order to reach the poorest groups in an increasingly diverse poverty situation, however, it is necessary to use an increasing degree of individual targeting in distributing resources specifically allocated for poverty-reduction purposes as poverty becomes more scattered within and across regions. The resources now being spent for poverty reduction may reach the various beneficiary groups more effectively through the adoption of both regional and individual targeting approaches (see Figure 7.1). This also has important implications for the design of credit policy and programs for poverty reduction.

13) Government efforts to develop financial institutions should be coupled with *individual initiatives,* and *formal banking institutions* should be supplemented by free, yet internally well-supervised and well-managed *informal organizations* for the poor (von Braun, Malik, and Zeller, 1993). Since the 1980s, the Agriculture Bank of China and Credit Cooperatives have supported the development of poor rural areas with their broadly distributed organizational networks. The ongoing credit programs for poverty reduction support about 100 million poor people; these programs improve food security, promote economic growth in the poor regions, and create a number of employment opportunities (He Linxiang, 1994.), but the programs have not directly integrated the poor.

Figure 7.1 Design of Mechanisms for Delivering Development-Assistance Resources

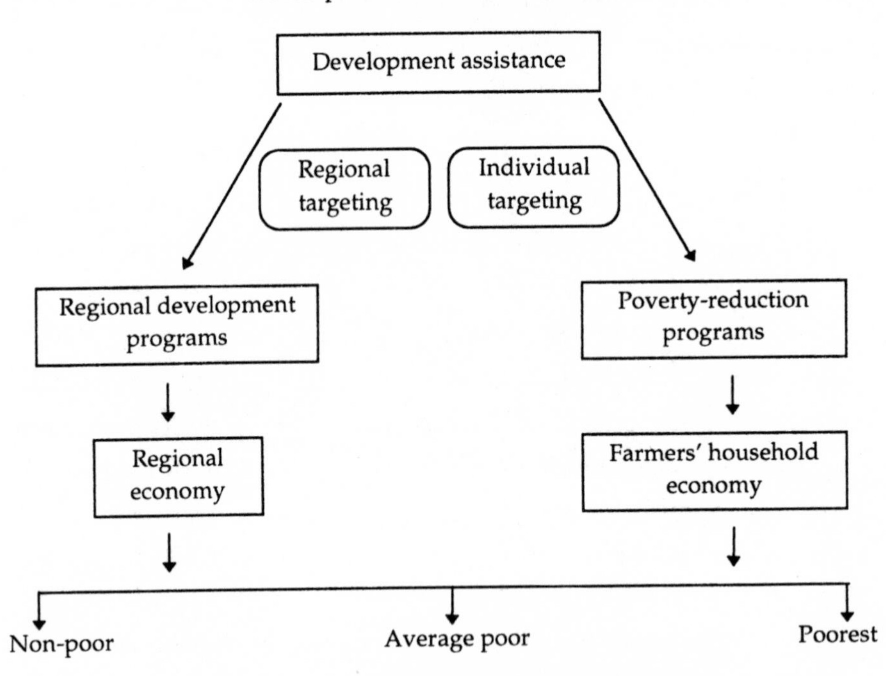

4. Learning From Others' Experiences and Further Experiments in China

14) It is increasingly realized that development policy goals would not be achieved if assistance were limited merely to funds and materials, without the formation and building of institutions. A variety of institutional experiments have been carried out in other developing countries with credit programs. Such innovative programs are of interest for China in reconsidering its approaches to the use of credit in its own anti-poverty policies and programs. These are also appropriate areas for China to seek international cooperation. In this respect, China might learn from the experiences of other nations and adapt such experiences to its local requirements.

15) It is noteworthy that there are a variety of informal organizations which provide credit for the poor, such as self-help credit groups, credits cooperatives and even banks of the poor in other developing countries, for instance in Bangladesh. These *innovative credit programs have yielded* successful experience in terms of micro lending to the poor and high rates of loan recovery (Yaron, 1992).[7] Similar experiments are also underway in China, such as mutual assistance credit groups and women's credit groups, etc., but they need to be studied further and supported.

16) The anti-poverty programs in various sectors should complement one other in order to achieve optimal effectiveness in promoting poverty-reducing economic growth, building on complementarities between the programs. Credit programs can therefore be designed to *link the advancement of agricultural technological extension*, cooperative movement in supply and marketing, and non-agricultural development schemes.

5. Integrating the Poorest in New Institutions

17) While the non-poor and average households are considered to be the first ones benefited by official credit programs for poverty reduction, some informal financing organizations represented by the Mutual Assistance Credit Groups have also integrated the poorest groups into the credit service systems in China. These organizations have been able to link the financing systems with social security systems at the village level, and combine disasters mitigation with poverty-reduction efforts by performing part of the relief functions of government institutions.

---

[7] see Zeller, M., et al.

18) In the credit business, the Mutual Assistance Credit Groups should effectively *link credit utilization with savings mobilization* and support their business operations mainly through their own resources. Rates of loan repayment improve as the responsibility of the members increases, as does also the initiative of the management to collect repayments. Moreover, the members of the groups can effectively supervise credit utilization themselves, which is helpful for loan recovery.

19) Credit programs ought to be designed with a component promoting *women's development*. It is suggested that women should be given priority as partners and beneficiaries in the implementation of credit projects. This does not imply any discrimination against men, but merely reflects that it is far more difficult for women to participate in the current credit system, and that overcoming this disadvantage will be beneficial to economic development in general, and women's participation in it.

20) The practice of the Mutual Assistance Credit Groups at village level has demonstrated effective solutions for two difficult problems encountered in implementing credit programs for poverty reduction, i.e. those of targeting poor groups and of guaranteeing loan repayments.

6. Linking and Freeing Informal Financial Institutions

21) It should also be pointed out, however, that informal credit organizations have been very weak in terms of capital accumulation. The impact of these organizations on rural economic growth and development will continue to be limited as long as the organiza-

tions remain weak. Their weakness, however, is partly a result of the legal restrictions under which they operate. Reform of the legal frameworks is needed in order to strengthen them.

22) The existing institutional capacities in China's rural financial system can and must be utilized effectively in any new institutional design for rural credit. This can best be achieved by creating *new linkages* between financial institutions and at the same time according them *greater independence*. As one step in this direction, it is necessary to set up *institutional linkages between Agriculture Banks / Credit Cooperatives and Mutual Assistance Credit Groups* to take advantage of the complementary effects of their respective organizational advantages, the formal and the informal credit institutions.

23) In cases where Village Credit Stations exist, Agriculture Banks and Credit Cooperatives can still reach rural households through the services of the Credit Stations. Otherwise, the two formal financing institutions would do better to release loans to the Mutual Assistance Groups or other cooperatives (see Figure 7.2) and let them handle the business of efficiently providing small-scale loans meet the consumption and production needs of the poor.

24) As a pre-condition for keeping such a comprehensive system in operation, the state should authorize the Agriculture Banks and Credit Cooperatives to *lend at market interest rates* to informal organizations, while the *informal organizations should be permitted to make their own decisions* regarding interest rates on their savings and credit business within the groups. In this indirect way, the state could help these informal groups become self-sustaining and to increase their effectiveness in delivering the needed development assistance to target groups.

25) Furthermore, it is necessary to strengthen the capacities of local group agents to implement credit programs, since they are more effective than any other external organization's agents for *training* and helping the poor to make the best use of credit services. These local group agents also will be in need for training in banking and project appraisal in order to become effective partners both to the poor and to the banking institutions. Government and banks will play important roles in facilitating such training.

Figure 7.2 Design of the Credit-Service Network at the Grass-Roots Level of Rural China

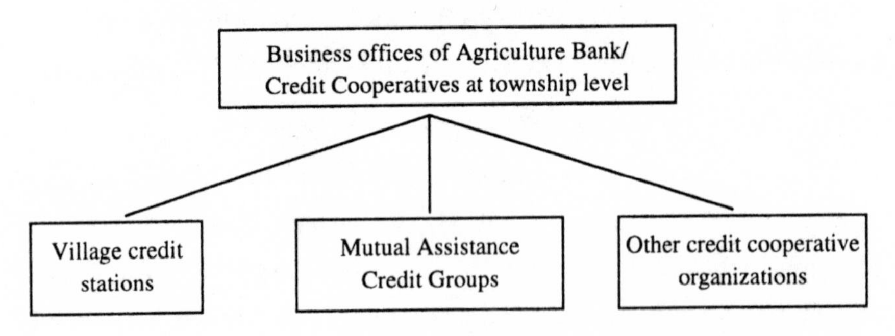

REFERENCES

Agricultural Development Bank of China (1994) *Constitution of the Agricultural Development Bank,* April 19, Beijing.

Asian and Pacific Regional Agricultural Credit Association, and Economic and Social Commission for Asia and the Pacific (1984) *Agricultural Credit and Banking System in China,* Bangkok: APRACA/ESCAP, CHINA 332.71 As 382a no. 12.

Braun, J. von, Malik, S. and Zeller, M. (1993) *Credit Markets, Input Support Policies, and the Poor: Insights from Africa and Asia,* Research paper presented in the Workshop "Post-Green Revolution Agricultural Development Strategies in the Third World: What Next?", July 30-31, Orlando, Florida.

Binswanger, H. P. and M. R. Rosenzweig (1986) *Behavioral and Material Determinants of Production Relation in Agriculture,* in Journal of Development Studies 22, London.

Chen Junsheng (1994) *Fight with Absolute Poverty,* in the Journal of "Development And Common Wealth", a specific publication for in memory of the International Day on Poverty Elimination, October 17, Beijing.

Chen Shaohua and M.Ravallion (1995) *Data in Transition: Assessing Rural Living Standards in Southern China,* Policy Research Department, World Bank, Washington DC.

Division of Monetary Reforms, the People's Bank of China (1991) *Monetary System Reforms of China,* Publishing House of Chinese Finance, Beijing.

Du Xiaoshan, Sun Ruomei and Xu Xianmei (1995) *Grameen Bank Model And Chinese Cooperatives for Poverty reduction,* in " Human Resource Development", no. 4, Beijing.

He Dexu (1995) *Monetary Reforms in China: Review for 1994 and Forward Looking to 1995,* in Economic Information", no. 3, Beijing.

He Linxiang (1994) *To Promote the Realization of the National Anti-poverty Plan for the Yeas of 1994-2000,* in the Journal of "Development And Common Wealth", no. 5, Beijing.

Hoff, K. and J. E. Stiglitz (1990) *Introduction: Imperfect Information and Rural Credit Markets - Puzzles and Policy Perspectives.* World Bank Economic Review 3 (September), Washington D.C.

Hong Fuzeng (1992) *Profile of Development of Rural Cooperative Foundations in China,* in Selective of Papers Presented in A International Workshop On Development of Cooperative Foundations in Rural China, Statistics Publishing House of China, Beijing.

Institute for Rural Development, Academy of Social Sciences, and Division of Rural Socioeconomic Statistics, State Statistics Bureau (1994) *Annual Report on Rural Economic Development of China in 1993,* Publishing House of Chinese Social Sciences , Beijing.

Kropp, E. and Marx, M.T., et al, (1989) *Linking Self-help Groups and Banks in Developing Countries,* published by Asian and Pacific Regional Agricultural Credit Association, and Deutsche Gesellschaft fuer Technische Zusammenarbeit GmbH, Eschborn.

Li Jianguang and Li Guo (1992) *Utilization of the Funds for Poverty reduction And Economic Development,* a research report submitted to the Ford Foundation, Beijing.

Lin Yifu (1992) *Institutions, Technologies, and Rural Development of China,* Shanghai Sanlian Bookstore, Shanghai.

Mayer, T. et al (1990) *Money, Banking, And the Economy* (a Chinese Translation), Shanghai Sanlian Bookstore, Shanghai.

Office of the Leading Groups of the State Council for Economic Development in Poor Areas (1989a) *Outlines of Economic Development in China's Poor Areas,* Agricultural Publishing House, Beijing.

Office of the Leading Group of the State Council for Economic Development in Poor Areas (1989b) *Document Compile on Economic Developments of Poor Areas,* People's Publishing House, Beijing.

Office of the Leading Group of the State Council for Economic Development in Poor Areas (1993) *A Profile on Economic Development and Poverty reduction* (a working report), September 15, Beijing.

Office of the Leading Group of the State Council for Economic Development in Poor Areas (1994a) *A Analysis Report on the 1993 Statistics of the Poor Counties,* September 23, Beijing.

Office of the Leading Group of the State Council for Economic Development in Poor Areas (1994b) *A Comprehensive Report on Statistics for Monitoring Projects of Poor Counties of China,* Beijing.

Ravallion, M. (1994) *Poverty Comparisons,* Harwood Academic Publishers, Singapore.

Ravallion, M., Chen Shaohua and J. Jalan (1996) *Dynamics of Poverty in Rural China,* Some Results from a World Bank Research Project, World Bank Resident Mission, Beijing.

Riskin, C. (1993) *Income Distribution and Poverty in Rural China,* in Griffin, K and Zhao Renwei ed. The Distribution of Income in China, p135-70, Macmillan Press LTD, London.

Policy Research Office of the Central Committee of the Chinese Communist Party and the Office for Rural Lang-standing observation network under the Ministry of Agriculture (1992) *compile on National Rural Socioeconomic Survey Data,* p.20, the Publishing House of the Central Party School, Beijing.

Schmidt. R. H. and Kropp E. (1987) ed. *Rural Finance Guiding Principles,* TZ - Verlagsgesellschaft mbH, Rossdorf.

The Central Committee of the Chinese Communist Party and the State Council (1996) *The Resolution on Solving Problems of Food and Cloth of the Rural Poor,* 23 October, Beijing.

The General Headquarters of the Agriculture Bank of China, (1987) *the Report with Regards to Improvement of Utilization of Subsidized Credits Specific for Poverty reduction,* October 16, Beijing.

The Agriculture Bank of China (1988) *Improving Rural Financial Services to Support Economic Development of Poor Areas* (a working report), February, Beijing.

The Leading Group of the State Council for Economic Development of Poor Areas (1986) *The Summary of the 3rd Plenary Meeting,* September 20, Beijing.

The Leading Group of the State Council for Economic Development (1989a) *the Regulations for Management on Economic Entities for Poverty Reduction,* February 13, Beijing.

The Leading Group of the State Council for Economic Development (1989b) *the Summary of the 7th Plenary Meeting,* February 1, Beijing.

The Ministry for Civil Affairs (1994) *A Document Compile on Mutual Assistance Credit Groups,* Social Publishing House of china, Beijing.

The People's Bank of China and The Agriculture Bank of China, (1986) *the Temporary Regulations on the Management of the Specially Subsidized Credits to the Poor Areas,* November 7 , Beijing .

The State Council (1994) *National Planning on Poverty Reduction for the Years of 1994-2000,* Beijing.

The State Statistics Bureau (1994) *The statistical yearbook of China*, pp. 543-549, The Statistics Publishing House, Beijing.

World Bank (1992) *China: Strategies for Reducing Poverty in the 1990s*, Washington DC.

Wu Qiang (1990) ed. *China: Rural Monetary Reforms And Development*, Financial and Economic Publishing House of China, Beijing.

Wu Guodong (1994) *Research Report on Credit Policies for Poverty reduction, presented in the International Workshop on Anti-poverty Strategies of China*, 4-7th of December, Beijing.

Xie Ping and Xu Jian, et al, (1992) *Financial Development And Monetary Reforms in China*, Tianjin People's Publishing House, Tianjin.

Xu Xiaobo and Deng Yingtao, et al, (1994) *Reforms And Development of Rural Financial Sector in China*, Contemporary China's Publishing House, Beijing.

Zeller, M., C. Schrieder, J. von Braun, F. Heidhues (1997). Rural Finance and Food Security for the Poor: Concept, Review and Implications for Research and Policy. Food Policy Review. International Food Policy Research Institute, Washington D.C. (forthcoming).

Zeller, M. A. Ahmed, S. Babu, S. Broca, A. Diagne, M. Sharma (1995) Rural Financial Policies for Food Security of the Poor: Methodologies for a Multicountry Research Project, International Food Policy Research Project, Washington D.C., FCND Discussion Paper II.

Zhang Xiaoshan and Wan Peng (1991) *Cooperative Theories and Practice*, City Publishing House of China, Beijing.

Zhou Binbin (1991) *Poverty Issues in the Period of People's Communes*, Economic Development Forums, no.3, Beijing.

Zhou Zhengqing (1994) *Socialist Market Economy And Monetary Reforms,* in Compile of Documents on Credit Management Reforms, Economic Publishing House of China, Beijing.

Zhu Ling and Jiang Zhongyi (1994) *Public Works And Poverty Reduction.* Shanghai: San Lian Bookstore and Shanghai People's Publishing House.

Zhu Ling and Jiang Zhongyi (1996) *Public Works and Poverty Alleviation in Rural China,* Nova Science Publishers, Inc. New York.

Zhu Ling, Jiang Zhongyi, Joachim von Braun (1996) (ed.), Credit for the Rural Poor in China. Proceedings of a Workshop held in Beibei, China. Beijing, Kiel (in Chinese and English).

Zhu Ling (1995a) *Why Do the Rural Women Not Make Decisions?* in "Human Resource Development" No. 4, Beijing.

Zhu Ling (1995b) *A Healthy Policy Bank - KfW of Germany,* in "Financial Research", no. 9, Beijing.

Zhu Ling (1996) *Effects of the Institutional Building on Implementation of the Poverty Reduction Schemes,* in "Economic Research", no. 4, Beijing.

INDEX

N

O

P

Q

R

S

T

U